Rosie's Secondary Market Price Guide for Charming Tails™

Editor and Collector: Rosalie "Rosie" J. Wells
Published by Rosie Wells Enterprises, Inc.
22341 E. Wells Rd.
Canton, IL 61520
Phone: 309/668-2211 Fax: 309/668-2795

Visit us on the internet!
http://www.RosieWells.com

Table of Contents

From the Editor III
About the Artist IV
About the Author V
Where It All Began VI
How to Use This Guide X

The Charming Tails™ Collection

    Charming Tails 1
    Easter/Spring 18
    Lazy Days 25
    The Wedding 28
    Tricks & Treats 31
    Giving Thanks 35
    Christmas Parade 44
    Deck the Halls 47
    Nativity 66
    Choo Choo 68
    Squashville 70
    Trim a Tree/Squashville 79
    Waterglobes 90
    Club 96
    Added Attractions 98
    Accessories 102
    San Francisco Music Co. 104
    Giftware by Silvestri 106
    Giftware by Roman 114

    RETIREMENTS 122
    INDEX 125
    NOTES

II

From the Editor

Charming Tails™... the name says it all! Each little animal figurine evokes a story which old and young alike can appreciate. Who cannot appreciate a relaxing walk in the woods to observe the small creatures which inhabit them? The artist and creator of Charming Tails, Dean Griff, has taken that walk and, with his talent, has created a view into this world; a view of the endearing inhabitants of Squashville. Adding humor and imagination, Dean Griff has given new meaning to the word enchantment. Each li'l creature of the woods becomes alive with personality.

I have met Dean Griff and found him to be just like the collection he creates... charming, to say the least! I wish him only continued success with Charming Tails and Fitz and Floyd.

I have enjoyed Charming Tails Collection since its early beginnings with Silvestri. And, as my collection has increased, unfortunately, time to do research for the guide has not! Research and thorough knowledge of a collection is essential in doing a guide. I feel very fortunate to have been able to work with Cathy Hauk to bring you, the collector, this Secondary Market Price Guide for Charming Tails. Her articles are a regular feature of the *Collectors' Bulletin*™. Many of you have known and met Cathy at numerous collector shows across the country. Her giggle is infectious as she delightfully tells about her favorite collection, Charming Tails, and her favorite artist, Dean Griff.

Having Cathy living close by has given us many advantages in producing this guide, not only because of her knowledge of Charming Tails and its early beginning with Silvestri, but also her communication with Dean Griff, and having the knowledge of his early creations before or during the beginning of Charming Tails. Because of this, and the collectors need to know, this guide features some of Dean Griff's early work with Silvestri and Roman.

I thank Cathy for her vast knowledge, and for the research she has done to bring this guide to you, the avid Charming Tails Collector. Feel free to direct questions for Cathy in care of this office. We will see that she receives them.

About The Editor

Rosie Wells is known as the "Collecting Editor." She has collected a variety of things since childhood. She collects of many, many things... including Charming Tails. Rosie was the first to publish what are now known as Secondary Market Price Guides. They are recognized in most collectible circuits as the most accurate and complete guides published today.

Rosie published her first publication in 1983, because she felt there wasn't enough information available for avid collectors. That first newsletter was eight pages long... how times have changed!

Rosie Wells Enterprises now publishes the *Collector's Bulletin*™, several annual price guides, and the *Weekly Collectors' Gazette*™, as well as keeping up a hot line and a web site.

Rosie and her husband, Dave, live on the farm on which her business is based. Dave and Rosie have a son, Tim, and a daughter, Beth. They also have a grandson, Hunter, and a granddaughter, Sydnie. Along with all that, Dave and Rosie have hosted, and continue to host, collector shows across the United States.

Having all this to keep up with, plus continuing her passion as an avid collector, Rosie is certainly the "Collecting Editor!"

Dean Griff
Charming Tails Artist

Woodland creatures have been used to tell stories to children for years. Now, those same adorable "critters" are telling stories to adults, as well. They say a picture is worth a thousand words... well, these small sculptures must be worth a million! Each beautifully detailed figure tells a charming "tale" (imagine that) of the quiet, innocent lives led by the characters.

The creator of these characters is Dean Griff. He has a strong connection to animals because he spent his childhood, and most of his young adulthood, on a farm in rural Oneida, NY.

Unlike most of today's children, Dean didn't spend his time playing Sony Play Station or watching television. Instead, he spent many hours outside observing the animals.

At a young age, Dean began to realize that he was artistically inclined. He taught himself to draw and eventually this interest in art led him to a position as the Curator of the Syracuse University Art Collection.

He received awards for his wildlife art in university contests and also started a small ornament business. Mostly, though, the ornaments were given to friends and family as gifts.

It wasn't until Dean moved to Florida and began working in the film industry that he got his first break in the gift market. You see, for a while Dean worked in the art department on the set of "Super Boy", the TV show. He went to a party one night and met a woman who worked for Silvestri in product development. After seeing an ornament that he had made as a gift, she asked that he submit 12 drawings of whatever he wanted.

Having never really had any experience in the gift industry, Dean had a hard time deciding what to draw. But eventually, he just did what came naturally.

He said, "My grandfather always told me that the eyes are the windows to the soul. So when I sit down to draw, I usually start with the eyes. As I was looking at the eyes, they kind of reminded me of a mouse's eyes. So I drew a mouse around them. I did the first twelve drawings and sent them in." The next year, those drawings were made into ornaments, and they were Silvestri's best sellers.

Charming Tails, as they would be called, grew increasingly popular. Dean Griff is now famous for these heart-warming characters. Part of their appeal is the fact that they represent something most people think we've lost... innocence.

Dean has said, "What inspires me the most to design is really just everyday activities... It's just that sight of the innocence of children and animals. The relationship they have with each other make me want to go home and do some more drawings for Charming Tails, because it renews my faith that there's goodness in all of us."

That renewal of faith is what collectors see every time they look at one of Dean's creations. No wonder they are so much in demand.

Cathy Hauk

Author

Cathy provided information for each figurine and compiled researching for prices

I don't think anyone sets out to be a collector. It just happens to them, perhaps quietly while you sleep. I have collected a few things, but nothing has caught my attention like these little critters.

I have put quite a few miles on the car going to signings and Charming Tails™ events. Some weeks we eat, sleep and talk Charming Tails™. That isn't the only thing that goes on around here. Jeff and I are an old married couple. We have been married since I was eighteen years old, so you know what patience he has. Scott is 12 and a delightful kid that goes quietly on one adventure after another. His passion is fishing, so you can imagine what his favorite piece is. We are having lots of fun together!

We live in a small town, not far from Rosie. I went kicking and screaming into the computer age until we started building our new home. The house needed to be wheelchair accessible for me, and a friend told me about the Bulletin Boards on the internet... from there, it was all downhill!

I love talking to the great friends I've made online, and have even had the pleasure of meeting some of them in person. Quite a wonderful and strange life, for a retired nurse!

I'm glad you decided to join us in all the excitement over Dean Griff's Charming Tails™. I would love to hear from you about your collection. You can find us online or drop a note at Catrink@AOL.com or write me in care of Rosie Wells Enterprises, Inc., 22341 E. Wells Road Canton, IL 61520. I'm always glad to talk about Charming Tails™!

Now for the thanks... especially to Jeff and Scott, who go way above the call of duty when it comes to Charming Tails™ i.e. "Can we please stop?," "Just one more minute?," "I am on the computer" and "Can you believe Dean has done it again?" These phrases have become my entire vocabulary.

Rosie and Dave have been unbelievable... thanks to them in allowing me to do this guide and all the hours and work that went into getting it done. Last and, of course, just as important, thanks to my online friends who have put up with me trying to find out anything and everything I can about Charming Tails.

A special thank you to Glenn Hynran for the grapevine pictures and Beth Litke for the Roman Chipmunk waterglobe. Also thank you to my sister, Penny, for being a good sport so I can go to more "Tails" events.

Cathy Hauk
a.k.a. cat

Where It All Began

by Cathy Hauk

It began with a very "charming" man named Dean Griff. After meeting him, I have no doubt that you will agree, there is no better word to describe him. If you have the chance to meet Mr. Griff, take a little longer drive, go a little further out of the way and maybe even make a weekend out of it. You will not be sorry, I promise. He is a very special artist and his fans will be the first to tell you so. I have yet to meet a collector, store owner or representative that has anything but kind words to say about him, which makes us even more delighted with his success.

Dean Griff went to a Christmas party and brought an ornament that he had made for a friend. A representative from Silvestri just happened to be there and loved the design. She asked him to do 12 drawings of anything that he wanted. The designs were introduced into the line in 1991 and deemed a success. Thus began what thousands of new collectors have grown to love as **Charming Tails**. New collectors is an appropriate term to use, because even the older collectors seem to have started around 1993. It would have been nice to have seen the dragonfly or the baskets or that darned cheese waterglobe on the shelf for retail! That being the case, I am excited to be a collector, for a couple years now, of such a wonderful line. I can't think of one piece that doesn't bring a smile, a giggle or a quiet thought. They seem to appeal to people of all ages. The collectors I have met have been husbands and wives, parents and children. Don't fret if you are just discovering them; there are lots of retired ones to be found with a little searching. Also, there are a few secondary market dealers that will help if you can't find what you need. One of the best things about this line, besides its endearing charm, is the price. The retail cost is $10 to $35 for most pieces, with the exception of the large houses and the waterglobes.

Having said all this, here is hoping you enjoy looking at all the pieces in the Charming Tails line, and that the values give you some idea where to start when buying and insuring your collection. For the most part, use the old rule of thumb, "Buy what you like." Don't buy because they might be worth more later, and you will never be disappointed.

Now that I've told you how the line was started, I'll tell you how my collection began.

I was waiting in line to have a stein signed at South Bend, Indiana, when a very quiet, darling man started talking to my husband, Jeff, my son, Scott, and myself. He signed a button for all of us and we began to look around at all the wonderful pieces. We were very disappointed we couldn't buy the ones we wanted. When we purchased *High Flying Mackenzie,* the line became a favorite at our house. We learned there were some harder to find, and that is when we began looking around in stores on our travels. *Pumpkin Slide* was added to our collection as a birthday gift for Jeff, and he began collecting them. Then we met Dean a second time and, to our delight, he remembered us! Now I know that he remembers everyone, but...

We picked up a few more and, all of a sudden, there seemed to be an infestation! I don't know when or how, but Jeff says that somewhere along the line, he lost control of his collection and I took it over. I am not sure that is a fair assessment of the situation, but I do think that it has become a passion. The whole family is involved!

One collector friend had the forethought to buy an extra dragonfly, and I purchased it for Jeff as an anniversary gift. Another good friend helped me give him a crystal mouse bell for his birthday. Scott has *I Have A Question For You* put away, just in case he needs it someday and, of course, I have my favorites as well. I don't think I'll say which ones right now... I don't want to hurt any of the Squashville characters' feelings. Every piece is wonderful! Just pick it up, look it over and you will notice some detail that makes you feel "warm and fuzzy" inside.

The wonderful people I have met on Prodigy, America Online, at shows and signings, can't all be wrong. I have met some of the greatest people and I am pleased to call them friends. I am sure I can speak for all collectors when I say, "Thank you, Mr. Griff, for creating something we can all share!" Now sit down, have a cup of tea *and enjoy the read!*

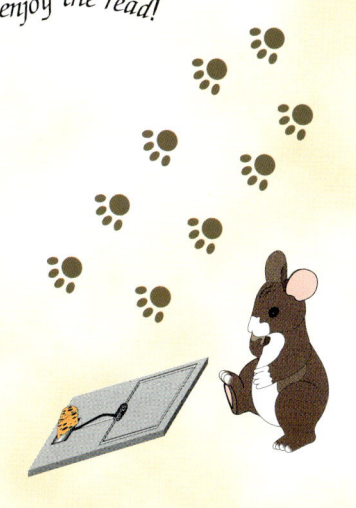

Let Me Set the Stage

First of all, you need a cast of characters. They are as follows: Mackenzie is the star mouse. Maxine is his girlfriend, and a mouse after my own heart. She likes to talk online (don't we all?), and if you haven't already heard, Mackenzie proposed! Maxine accepted and they were married the nineteenth of April, 1998.

Reginald is a raccoon. He has trouble with *Christmas Lights.* He used to sell papers but retired. Now I think that he is doing some *Drum Major* work.

Chauncey is a chipmunk. He has done some acorn seed disbursement in *One For You,* and was retired after *Peeking At Presents.* I suspect that the last incident is why they released baby pictures of him in *Chauncey's First Christmas.*

Binkey has been humiliated in public while being decorated; that could have been done more easily while he was taking a *Midday Snooze,* a *Gardening Break* or an *Afternoon Snooze.* He started out with *Love Blooms* along with his companion, Bunny, and *Guess What.*

Belle is the quietest of the whole bunch, *Catchin' ZZZ's* with Maxine or pulling a leaf sleigh.

Lydia seems to appear everywhere, from taking Mackenzie for a ride to sitting quietly on his head while he dreams of Maxine. She is the busiest with an anonymous snail, who is waiting for fans of Squashville to give him a name. Of course, there are occasional nameless visitors, such as an owl in a tree, a couple of gold finches and a turtle in the 1998 line.

VIII

The Leaf & Acorn Society

The Leaf & Acorn Society was the predecessor to the collectors' club. It was launched at Rosemont, IL, and extended to the Florida Extravaganza. It boasts a membership of approximately 1,500 lucky collectors that were allowed to keep their membership numbers if they joined the Leaf & Acorn Club. With their membership, they were given an official certificate, an Acorn Society tote bag, a cloisonné Mackenzie pin, *Hot Doggin'*, signed by Dean, and a pen.

The Leaf & Acorn Club

Just a quick note about the Leaf & Acorn Club; 1997 was its charter year, and it is growing by leaps and bounds after a bumpy start. *The Squashville Gazette* is the newsletter sent out by the club. Members receive a Charming Tails catalog, a club piece, and an opportunity to purchase Members Only pieces. If you are interested in joining, contact:

The Leaf & Acorn Club
P.O. Box 78218
St. Louis, MO 63178-8218
1-800-486-1065

The Charter Membership pieces were *Thank You* and a resin pin of the first Members Only piece, *Maxine's Leaf Collection*.

Giftware

This is the term that collectors have penned for the works Dean Griff designed before or during the early days of Charming Tails. The value on these are very subjective. There are people who collect only Charming Tails, and there are collectors who want anything they can find created by Dean Griff. So, as always, use your own judgement and buy what you like. Either way, you might be interested in the ornaments and figurines Dean Griff has created.

Hey! Where are the Production Marks?

If you are just starting to collect, things are getting better! The pieces are being marked and named on the bottom. This will help both the collector and the retailer know what pieces they have. At the present time, no mark is showing any indication of escalating prices. However, as time wears on, the older marks will probably be preferred. Here is how the markings work:

1998: Paw Print

1996: Acorn

1997: Maple Leaf

1995 or Older:
No Mark,
Gold Silvestri sticker made in China,
Roller Stamp Mark Silvestri or Felt Bottom

For Your Information

There are some pale or "naked" mice out there. These have a mistake in the painting technique, a result of miscommunication. They were supposed to be darker and antiqued. Due to a misunderstanding, there were also some pieces numbered that were not limited edition. One catalog mentioned the *Woodland Collection* by Dean Griff, the early Charming Tails line. Also, the original spelling of Mackenzie in a few publications was "Mickensey."

IX

How To Use This Guide

The pieces in this guide are listed in order, according to type and order number.

① **87399** ② **Taggin' Along** ③ ☐
④ ***RETIRED 1997***
⑤ *COMMENTS:* Issued 1996, *Original Retail:* $15.00
The little snail is found on a lot of pieces. This time he has *Mackenzie's* tail in his mouth.
⑥ **Sec. Mkt.: $20**
⑦ _____ Have _____ Want _____ Paid
⑧ _____

1. Style/order number.

2. Figurine's name or names.

3. Instant Alert – Do I or do I not have this piece? If this piece is a part of your collection, mark ✓ in the box.

4. If retired prior to press time, you'll be told in bold letters!

5. Comments: Contains year of introduction, editor's comments, differences, errors, etc. Each year's guide may contain added information, reporting variations, changes and new information from collectors, etc.

6. Use these secondary market prices as a "guide" to resell, buy or insure your collection. Some pieces have NE listed as the secondary market price. This means that the price has yet to be established due to the piece being recently introduced. Always do your own research, as prices may fluctuate from time to time.

7. Mark these spaces to record the price you paid and if you have or want this piece. Great for others to peek at for special gift giving!

8. By popular demand, a special line has been added for you to list your figurine's individual registration number.

Every effort has been made to assure this guide is complete and accurate. Use the prices in this guide only as a guide to help determine the piece value for insurance evaluation.

Charming Tails

87353   Surrounded By Friends
RETIRED 1997

COMMENTS: Issued 1996, *Original Retail:* $17.00

This piece has been found with blue flowers rather than pink flowers.

Sec. Mkt.: $18 - 28

_____ Have   _____ Want   _____ Paid

87357   Why Hello There
RETIRED 1997

COMMENTS: Issued 1996, *Original Retail:* $15.00

The butterfly is attached by a small wire.

Sec. Mkt.: $18 - 25

_____ Have   _____ Want   _____ Paid

87360   One For Me...
RETIRED 1997

COMMENTS: Issued 1996, *Original Retail:* $17.00

Confusing to remember which is which; *One For You* and *One For Me*. *One For Me* is Mackenzie and has only one pea. This piece appears to be hollow; much lighter in weight.

Sec. Mkt.: $20 - 35

_____ Have   _____ Want   _____ Paid

87361   One For You...
RETIRED 1997

COMMENTS: Issued 1996, *Original Retail:* $17.00

The way to remember which is which, is this is Chauncey and he is sharing... one for you, one for me....

Sec. Mkt.: $20 - 30

_____ Have   _____ Want   _____ Paid

Charming Tails

87362   Tuggin' Two-some
LIMITED EDITION OF 10,000

COMMENTS: Issued 1996, *Original Retail:* $18.00

Has been slowly picking up momentum and is just now beginning to get noticed for how cute it is.

Sec. Mkt.: $31 - 38

_____ Have   _____ Want   _____ Paid

87364   The Gardening Break

COMMENTS: Issued 1996, *Original Retail:* $17.00

The endearing part of Charming Tails is that you can just imagine finding the Squashville characters in these situations.

Sec. Mkt.: NE

_____ Have   _____ Want   _____ Paid

87365   I'm Full
RETIRED 1997

COMMENTS: Issued 1996, *Original Retail:* $16.00

The detail, like Binkey's full tummy, makes us all nostalgic for many a family feast.

Sec. Mkt.: $25 - 35

_____ Have   _____ Want   _____ Paid

87366   This Is Hot!
RETIRED 1997

COMMENTS: Issued 1996, *Original Retail:* $16.00

This piece is in Dean's pocket in the 1996 catalog.

Sec. Mkt.: $25 - 38

_____ Have   _____ Want   _____ Paid

87367   Hello, Sweet Pea
RETIRED 1997

COMMENTS: Issued 1996, *Original Retail:* $13.00

Mackenzie looks busy shelling peas, which brings back fond memories of a country afternoon.

Sec. Mkt.: $18 - 25

_____ Have   _____ Want   _____ Paid

Charming Tails

87369 Picking Peppers
RETIRED 1997
COMMENTS: Issued 1996, *Original Retail:* $13.00
Chauncey looks quite comfortable in this piece.
Sec. Mkt.: $20 - 25

_____ Have   _____ Want   _____ Paid

87384 The Waterslide
COMMENTS: Issued 1996, *Original Retail:* $21.00
Collectors nervously waited when these began shipping, wondering if there would be enough for everyone. You can see why it delighted them.
Sec. Mkt.: $27 - 35

_____ Have   _____ Want   _____ Paid

87390 I'm Berry Happy
RETIRED 1997
COMMENTS: Issued 1996, *Original Retail:* $16.00
Binkey must have a sweet tooth. You can also find him in a strawberry and a basket of berries.
Sec. Mkt.: $25 - 30

_____ Have   _____ Want   _____ Paid

87391 The Berry Best
RETIRED 1997
COMMENTS: Issued 1996, *Original Retail:* $17.00
There is also a musical by San Francisco Music Box Company.
Sec. Mkt.: $20 - 28

_____ Have   _____ Want   _____ Paid

87395 You Love Me – You Love Me Not
COMMENTS: Issued 1996, *Original Retail:* $17.00
The flower pieces look great in a scene!
Sec. Mkt.: NE

_____ Have   _____ Want   _____ Paid

Charming Tails

87396 Take Time To Reflect
RETIRED 1997
COMMENTS: Issued 1996, *Original Retail:* $17.00

Stewart looks especially nice with *Waterslide* and *Cattail Catapult*.

Sec. Mkt.: $20 - 30

_____ Have   _____ Want   _____ Paid

87398 Training Wings
RETIRED 1997
COMMENTS: Issued 1996, *Original Retail:* $17.00

A lot of the pieces were found with the little mouse broken off the pole.

Sec. Mkt.: $18 - 25

_____ Have   _____ Want   _____ Paid

87399 Taggin' Along
RETIRED 1997
COMMENTS: Issued 1996, *Original Retail:* $15.00

The little snail is found on a lot of pieces. This time he has Mackenzie's tail in his mouth.

Sec. Mkt.: $20 - 28

_____ Have   _____ Want   _____ Paid

87423 Catchin' Butterflies
COMMENTS: Issued 1996, *Original Retail:* $17.00

This was also released in a musical by San Francisco Music Box Company. This was one of only two pieces which had big wide eyes.

Sec. Mkt.: $25 - 28

_____ Have   _____ Want   _____ Paid

87425 Hoppity Hop
RETIRED 1997
COMMENTS: Issued 1996, *Original Retail:* $15.00

Binkey is attached by a spring.

Sec. Mkt.: $18 - 25

_____ Have   _____ Want   _____ Paid

Charming Tails

87448 Cattail Catapult

COMMENTS: Issued 1996, *Original Retail:* $17.00

This piece has been found with the snail facing the opposite direction. While not a limited edition, this piece is harder to find.

Sec. Mkt.: $20

_____ Have   _____ Want   _____ Paid

84525 Mouse In Apple Box (*Set of 3*)
RETIRED 1994

COMMENTS: Issued 1994, *Original Retail:* $15.00

Wooden nesting box that has a large mouse painted on the outside, like a color book drawing. The rear of the mouse is on the back, the middle nesting box is painted with a mouse also and the third is a tiny apple. Sizes are 3", 2", and 1", respectively.

Sec. Mkt.: $50 - 85

_____ Have   _____ Want   _____ Paid

89190 Maxine's Butterfly Ride
RETIRED 1996

COMMENTS: Issued 1995, *Original Retail:* $16.50

This piece is especially adorable, and its future might be worth watching. You know what happened to the other bugs! Found in earlier catalogs as *Mouse On Butterfly*.

Sec. Mkt.: $30 - 40

_____ Have   _____ Want   _____ Paid

89191 Mouse On Bee
RETIRED 1994

COMMENTS: Issued 1994, *Original Retail:* $10.00

This is affectionately known as one of the bugs and is one of the most sought after. When you see it, you will see how delightful it is.

Sec. Mkt.: $225 - 300

_____ Have   _____ Want   _____ Paid

Charming Tails

89305 Binkey In A Lily ☐
RETIRED 1996

COMMENTS: Issued 1995, *Original Retail* $16.00

This is a very pretty piece, and the only one where Binkey is not gray. The collectors noticed this detail and it was retired. Hopefully, there will be more of this black bunny in the line; he is gorgeous! *Binkey In A Lily* has been found in various shades of color. Found in earlier catalogs as *Bunny In A Lily*.

Sec. Mkt.: $45 - 60

_____ Have   _____ Want   _____ Paid

89306 Two Peas In A Pod ☐
RETIRED 1996

COMMENTS: Issued 1995, *Original Retail*: $14.00

Hello Sweet Pea makes a nice companion piece. Found in earlier catalogs as *Two Peas In A Pod Mice*.

Sec. Mkt.: $30 - 40

_____ Have   _____ Want   _____ Paid

89307 Hide And Seek ☐
RETIRED 1994

COMMENTS: Issued 1994, *Original Retail*: $13.50

More than one collector has been confused by the similarities of this piece and *Binkey's New Pal*. The difference is two mice instead of a bunny and a ladybug. Found in earlier catalogs as *Hide And Seek Mice*.

Sec. Mkt.: $175 - 200

_____ Have   _____ Want   _____ Paid

89310 Spring Flowers/Yellow Flower ☐
RETIRED 1996

COMMENTS: Issued 1994, *Original Retail*: $16.00

The yellow flower has a tiny acrylic dew drop falling from the tulip. It is also a musical from San Francisco Music Box Company. Found in earlier catalogs as *Mice With Flowers*.

Sec. Mkt.: $45 - 65

_____ Have   _____ Want   _____ Paid

Charming Tails

89310 Spring Flowers/Blue Flower
RETIRED 1996

COMMENTS: Issued 1994, *Original Retail:* $16.00

The yellow flower and blue flower are both issued under the same item number.

Sec. Mkt.: $45 - 60

_____ Have   _____ Want   _____ Paid

89312 Rabbit/Daffodil

RETIRED 1995

COMMENTS: Issued 1994, *Original Retail:* $13.50 ea.

The bunny on this one is different than *Binkey*. He seems to be an older looking bunny and his coloring is more brown. In one variation the rabbit faces the candle. On the other variation the rabbit faces away from the candle.

Sec. Mkt.: $175 - 200

_____ Have   _____ Want   _____ Paid

89314 Love Mice
RETIRED 1994

COMMENTS: Issued 1994, *Original Retail:* $15.00

Check out the mice tails on *Love Mice*. They are made of rubber with wire inside.

Sec. Mkt.: $75 - 125

_____ Have   _____ Want   _____ Paid

Charming Tails

89318   King Of The Mushroom
RETIRED 1996

COMMENTS: Issued 1995, *Original Retail:* $16.00

One of the recently retired pieces, this is quickly escalating on the secondary market. Found in earlier catalogs as *Bunny On Mushroom*.

Sec. Mkt.: $36 - 50

_____ Have   _____ Want   _____ Paid

89320   Mouse On Dragonfly
RETIRED 1994

COMMENTS: Issued 1994, *Original Retail:* $16.50

This is probably the most sought after piece of all the *Charming Tails*. Most retailers that had them initially said they didn't like them and they had a lot of breakage. Good luck finding one, even at the secondary market price! Also found in a pale version.

Sec. Mkt.: $300 - 325

_____ Have   _____ Want   _____ Paid

89321   Mouse on Grasshopper
RETIRED 1994

COMMENTS: Issued 1994, *Original Retail:* $15.00

This is the cutest of the bugs! *Mackenzie* is holding a little purple flower. May be found with lighter colored mice.

Sec. Mkt.: $110 - 150

_____ Have   _____ Want   _____ Paid

89558   After Lunch Snooze
RETIRED

COMMENTS: Issued 1994, *Original Retail:* $16.00

The mouse and bunny are very small on this. This piece sold out in 1997.

Sec. Mkt.: $33 - 40

_____ Have   _____ Want   _____ Paid

Charming Tails

89560   Slumber Party
RETIRED 1996

COMMENTS: Issued 1995, *Original Retail:* $16.00

The Goldfinch is taking care of her young and a napping *Mackenzie*.

Sec. Mkt.: $45 - 60

_____ Have   _____ Want   _____ Paid

89563   Springtime Showers
RETIRED 1996

COMMENTS: Issued 1995, *Original Retail:* $10.00 ea.

Listed with the same item number, *Binkey*, *Reginald* and *Mackenzie* each hang from a 5" long acrylic raindrop. These are very nice, especially in a window. They reflect a little bit of light.

Sec. Mkt.: $30 - 45

_____ Have   _____ Want   _____ Paid

Charming Tails

89586 Binkey's New Pal
RETIRED 1996

COMMENTS: Issued 1995, *Original Retail:* $14.00

A great companion piece to *Hide and Seek*, they make new collectors crazy until they figure out the difference. This piece sold out in 1996!

Sec. Mkt.: $27 - 35

_____ Have   _____ Want   _____ Paid

89601 Fragile Handle With Care
LIMITED EDITION OF 15,000

COMMENTS: Issued 1997, *Original Retail:* $19.00

This piece was mistakenly issued as *Love Doesn't Come With Instructions*. The only difference is the understamp. *Love Doesn't Come With Instructions* had approximately 1,500 produced. These were numbered and marked with an Acorn mark. *Fragile Handle With Care*, was numbered and marked with an Acorn mark. There were approximately 1,728 *Fragile Handle With Care* without registration numbers. They forgot to add the registration number when the year of production mark was changed.

Some found with elusive blue diamond. Found in earlier catalogs as *Love Don't Come with Instructions*.

Sec. Mkt.: *Fragile Handle With Care*: **$25 - 40**

Fragile Handle With Care **(No Reg. Number): $50 - $75**

Love Doesn't Come With Instructions: **$50 - 75**

_____ Have   _____ Want   _____ Paid

Charming Tails

89603   I Have A Question For You ☐
COMMENTS: Issued 1997, *Original Retail:* $17.00
I put one away. Who knows? Perhaps for a future daughter-in-law!
Sec. Mkt.: NE

_____ Have   _____ Want   _____ Paid

89608   Flower Friends ☐
COMMENTS: Issued 1997, *Original Retail:* $16.00
This is one of my favorites! I love the lavender Iris. Found with blue Iris also.
Sec. Mkt.: $25 - 35

_____ Have   _____ Want   _____ Pad

89617   Midday Snooze ☐
COMMENTS: Issued 1997, *Original Retail:* $19.00
This is also a musical from San Francisco Music Box Company.
Sec. Mkt.: NE

_____ Have   _____ Want   _____ Paid

89619   Bunny Buddies ☐
COMMENTS: Issued 1997, *Original Retails:* $21.00
The piece pictured in the 1997 catalog showed the bunnies in two different colors. However, it was shipped with two gray bunnies. The only one known as pictured was a prototype sold at the Flamingo Fling in Florida, in 1996.
Sec. Mkt.: NE

_____ Have   _____ Want   _____ Paid

89623   Hangin' Around ☐
COMMENTS: Issued 1997, *Original Retail:* $16.00
Mackenzie and *Maxine* seem to be playing in the flowers. Can you tell which is which?
Sec. Mkt.: NE

_____ Have   _____ Want   _____ Paid

Charming Tails

89624   Ahhh-Chooo! ☐
COMMENTS: Issued 1997, *Original Retail:* $13.00
Can't you sympathize with poor *Chauncey's* allergies?
Sec. Mkt.: NE

_____ Have   _____ Want   _____ Paid

89625   You Couldn't Be Sweeter ☐
COMMENTS: Issued 1997, *Original Retail:* $17.00
This is a great companion piece to *Fragile Handle With Care.*
Sec. Mkt.: NE

_____ Have   _____ Want   _____ Paid

89626   I See Things Clearly Now ☐
COMMENTS: Issued 1997, *Original Retail:* $15.00
Try setting this one up so you can look through the looking glass to see *Mackenzie.* You'll be delighted!
Sec. Mkt.: NE

_____ Have   _____ Want   _____ Paid

89627   Plane Friends ☐
COMMENTS: Issued 1997, *Original Retail:* $19.00
This is a big hit with the little boys!
Sec. Mkt.: NE

_____ Have   _____ Want   _____ Paid

89703   There's No "Us" Without "U" ☐
COMMENTS: Issued 1998, *Original Retail:* $19.50
Binkey and *Bunny* are holding alphabet blocks with the letters "u" and "s" on them.
Sec. Mkt.: NE

_____ Have   _____ Want   _____ Paid

Charming Tails

89704   It's Your Move   □
COMMENTS: Issued 1998, *Original Retail:* $17.00

Mackenzie with a black and white pawn on a chess tile. A great piece for a chess player and for the "masculine" collector.

Sec. Mkt.: NE

_____ Have   _____ Want   _____ Paid

89705   Even The Ups And Downs Are Fun! □
COMMENTS: Issued 1998, *Original Retail:* $16.50

Maxine is on a yo-yo; *Mackenzie* is laying beside the yo-yo.

Sec. Mkt.: NE

_____ Have   _____ Want   _____ Paid

89706   I'm Here For You   □
COMMENTS: Issued 1998, *Original Retail:* $17.50

Mackenzie comforts *Maxine*.

Sec. Mkt.: NE

_____ Have   _____ Want   _____ Paid

89713   How Many Candles?   □
COMMENTS: Issued 1998, *Original Retail:* $16.50

The first prototype had too many candles. Production was changed to a white cake.

Sec. Mkt.: NE

_____ Have   _____ Want   _____ Paid

Charming Tails

89716   Steady Wins The Race
1998 LIMITED EDITION

COMMENTS: Issued 1998, *Original Retail:* $20.00

The finish line is in sight. *Binkey* is catching a ride on a new character's back... the turtle. The turtle is sure to be a hit with collectors. Look for this to be a sell out! Some have been found with Lydia going the wrong direction.

Sec. Mkt.: $25

_____ Have   _____ Want   _____ Paid

89717   Hear, Speak, See No Evil

COMMENTS: Issued 1998, *Original Retail:* $17.50

Maybe these little fellows know the secret of *Charming Tails* yet to come.

Sec. Mkt.: NE

_____ Have   _____ Want   _____ Paid

89719   I'm A Winner

COMMENTS: Issued 1998, *Original Retail:* $16.00

Everyone has a system for picking numbers. This one has a special significance to a *Charming Tails* person. Just ask Dean.

Sec. Mkt.: NE

_____ Have   _____ Want   _____ Paid

89720   A Little Bird Told Me So

COMMENTS: Issued 1998, *Original Retail:* $17.00

Collectors have been pleading for more birds. Looks like someone was listening!

Sec. Mkt.: NE

_____ Have   _____ Want   _____ Paid

89722   Picture Perfect

COMMENTS: Issued 1998, *Original Retail:* $17.50

Maxine wears flowers or some kind of decoration in all the new introductions. So now we know who is who!

Sec. Mkt.: NE

_____ Have   _____ Want   _____ Paid

Charming Tails

97715　Happy Birthday

COMMENTS: Issued 1996, *Original Retail:* $16.00

Poor *Mackenzie* can't believe he ate the whole thing! A candle flame has been shown in yellow and orange. This piece is becoming difficult to locate.

Sec. Mkt.: $25

_____ Have　　_____ Want　　_____ Paid

97716　Good Luck

COMMENTS: Issued 1996, *Original Retail:* $16.00

This is a great piece for St. Patrick's Day.

Sec. Mkt.: $20

_____ Have　　_____ Want　　_____ Paid

97717　New Arrival

COMMENTS: Issued 1996, *Original Retail:* $16.50

This is a wonderful piece for a new baby, though more difficult to locate!

Sec. Mkt.: $20

_____ Have　　_____ Want　　_____ Paid

97718　Reach For The Stars

COMMENTS: Issued 1996, *Original Retail:* $17.00

This is Dean's favorite piece! It was also issued in a music box by San Francisco Music Box Company.

Sec. Mkt.: $30 - 45

_____ Have　　_____ Want　　_____ Paid

97719　Get Well Soon
RETIRED 1997

COMMENTS: Issued 1996, *Original Retail:* $16.00

This piece was also marketed to hospital gift shops.

Sec. Mkt.: $20 - 45

_____ Have　　_____ Want　　_____ Paid

Charming Tails

97720 I'm So Sorry ☐
COMMENTS: Issued 1996, *Original Retail:* $16.50

The attention to detail on this piece is so enchanting! Notice the little tear on the mouse's cheek.

Sec. Mkt.: NE

_____ Have   _____ Want   _____ Paid

97721 It's Not The Same Without You ☐
RETIRED 1997

COMMENTS: Issued 1996, *Original Retail:* $16.00

There was a lot of breakage on this piece; however, many collectors fell in love with the sentiment of it.

Sec. Mkt.: $20 - 35

_____ Have   _____ Want   _____ Paid

97722 We'll Weather The Storm ☐
COMMENTS: Issued 1996, *Original Retail:* $16.50

This piece is wonderful, with the acrylic raindrops falling off the leaves. A few glass raindrops have been found.

Sec. Mkt.: NE

_____ Have   _____ Want   _____ Paid

97723 Hope You're Feeling Better ☐
RETIRED

COMMENTS: Issued 1996, *Original Retail:* $16.50

This is one of the pieces that is becoming hard to find. It was marketed to hospital gift shops. This piece sold out in 1997.

Sec. Mkt.: $20 - 40

_____ Have   _____ Want   _____ Paid

97724 I Love You ☐
COMMENTS: Issued 1996, *Original Retail:* $16.00

One of the few pieces produced with the eyes closed.

Sec. Mkt.: NE

_____ Have   _____ Want   _____ Paid

Charming Tails

98349 Binkey's First Cake
RETIRED 1997

COMMENTS: Issued 1995, *Original Retail:* $17.00

This was one of those sleeper pieces... people waited to purchase and found it was gone when they returned.

Sec. Mkt.: $40 - 45

_____ Have   _____ Want   _____ Paid

98460 Mender Of Broken Hearts
RETIRED 1996

COMMENTS: Issued 1996, *Original Retail:* $15.00

This a great piece for Valentine's Day; just add a handful of conversation hearts.

Sec. Mkt.: $38 - 45

_____ Have   _____ Want   _____ Paid

98461 How Do You Measure Love
RETIRED 1996

COMMENTS: Issued 1996, *Original Retail:* $15.00

Mackenzie is measuring love with a paper tapes measure.

Sec. Mkt.: $31 - 40

_____ Have   _____ Want   _____ Paid

Easter / Spring

87372 After The Hunt
COMMENTS: Issued 1996, *Original Retail:* $19.00

Binkey is just plain worn out after hunting for all of the Easter treasures.

Sec. Mkt.: $38 - 45

_____ Have _____ Want _____ Paid

87373 Look Out Below
RETIRED 1997

COMMENTS: Issued 1996, Original Retail: $21.00
This piece is becoming a little more difficult to find.

Sec. Mkt.: $25 - 30

_____ Have _____ Want _____ Paid

87377 Gathering Treats
COMMENTS: Issued 1996, *Original Retail:* $13.00

Lydia the ladybug is along for a ride on the jelly beans.

Sec. Mkt.: $30 - 38

_____ Have _____ Want _____ Paid

87379 Want A Bite?
RETIRED 1997

COMMENTS: Issued 1996, *Original Retail:* $19.00

The companion piece, *Wanna Play*, took off but this piece can still be found at retail with a little work.

Sec. Mkt.: $25 - 30

_____ Have _____ Want _____ Paid

Easter/Spring

87386   The Chase Is On
RETIRED 1997

COMMENTS: Issued 1996, *Original Retail:* $17.00

The motion on this piece is wonderful! You can just imagine poor Binkey running away.

Sec. Mkt.: $22 - 28

_____ Have   _____ Want   _____ Paid

87422   Binkey's Bouncing Bundle
LIMITED EDITION OF 17,500

COMMENTS: Issued 1996, *Original Retail:* $18.00

Binkey's Bouncing Bundle sold out in 1996. This may be a piece to watch for secondary market price increase in the future. Note: Egg in on spring and can be found in any direction.

Sec. Mkt.: $35 - 40

_____ Have   _____ Want   _____ Paid

87424   Bunny Love

COMMENTS: Issued 1996, *Original Retail:* $19.00

Binkey and Bunny seem quite content! This piece is more difficult to locate.

Sec. Mkt.: $25

_____ Have   _____ Want   _____ Paid

88600   What's Hatchin'?

COMMENTS: Issued 1997, *Original Retail:* $17.00

Chickie Back Ride, Can I Keep Him and *What's Hatchin* would make a great display!

Sec. Mkt.: $18

_____ Have   _____ Want   _____ Paid

88603   No Thanks, I'm Stuffed

COMMENTS: Issued 1997, *Original Retail:* $16.00

Binkey and Mackenzie are great feeding this stuffed pink bunny. Collectors did not like the eyes on neither toy, Binkey or Mackenzie.

Sec. Mkt.: NE

_____ Have   _____ Want   _____ Paid

Easter/Spring

88700 Chickie Back Ride

COMMENTS: Issued 1998, *Original Retail:* $16.00

Mackenzie rides the infamous little chick. This looks to be a sellout and is already more difficult to find; keep your eyes on it!

Sec. Mkt.: $20

_____ Have   _____ Want   _____ Paid

88701 Paint By Paws

COMMENTS: Issued 1998, *Original Retail:* $16.00

Binkey paints blue paw prints on an Easter egg while a blue paint tube overflows behind him. There are little pink flowers on the grass. This piece is also more difficult to find.

Sec. Mkt.: $20

_____ Have   _____ Want   _____ Paid

89313 Animals In Eggs/Yellow Chick
RETIRED 1996

COMMENTS: Issued 1995, *Original Retail:* $11.00

The yellow chick has only one wing! Of course, the other wing is tucked inside the eggshell.

Sec. Mkt.: $35 - 45

_____ Have   _____ Want   _____ Paid

89313 Animals In Eggs/Bunny
RETIRED 1996

COMMENTS: Issued 1995, *Original Retail:* $11.00

These look darling sitting in an egg carton for Easter.

Sec. Mkt.: $40 - 45

_____ Have   _____ Want   _____ Paid

89313 Animals In Eggs/Duck
RETIRED 1996

COMMENTS: Issued 1995, *Original Retail:* $11.00

There are four different styles of this piece; yellow chick, bunny, duck and mouse. All issued under the same item number.

Sec. Mkt.: $35 - 40

_____ Have   _____ Want   _____ Paid

Easter/Spring

89313 Animals In Eggs/Mouse
RETIRED 1996
COMMENTS: Issued 1995, *Original Retail:* $11.00
The mouse is the most desirable to most collectors.
Sec. Mkt.: $45 - 55

_____ Have   _____ Want   _____ Paid

89315 Duckling Votive
RETIRED 1994
COMMENTS: Issued 1994, *Original Retail:* $13.00
The eggshell holds a little glass votive and a little white candle.
Sec. Mkt.: $225 - 275

_____ Have   _____ Want   _____ Paid

89316 Duckling In Egg w/Mouse
RETIRED 1994
COMMENTS: Issued 1994, *Original Retail:* $15.00
This is another one of those difficult pieces to find, and I suspect they are sitting in the homes of people who don't know about *Charming Tails. I have seen only one for sale, therefore the value is very subjective.*
Sec. Mkt.: $300 - 325

_____ Have   _____ Want   _____ Paid

89317 Bunny w/Carrot Candleholder
RETIRED 1994
COMMENTS: Issued 1995, *Original Retail:* $12.00
This is a top-heavy piece. If you have it, use a small taper in it.
Sec. Mkt.: $82 - 100

_____ Have   _____ Want   _____ Paid

Easter/Spring

89559   Jelly Bean Feast
RETIRED 1996

COMMENTS: Issued 1995, *Original Retail:* $14.00

Mackenzie has definitely made a pig of himself! I think I'll put him in a bowl of jelly beans for display!

Sec. Mkt.: $27 - 35

_____ Have   _____ Want   _____ Paid

89561   Wanna Play?
LIMITED EDITION OF 2,500

COMMENTS: Issued 1995, *Original Retail:* $15.00

This piece *Wanna Play* was sold out in 1995. This is a great companion piece for *Wanna Bite*. There were definitely not enough of these to go around. You're probably going to have to find this one on the secondary market.

Sec. Mkt.: $175 - 185

_____ Have   _____ Want   _____ Paid

89600   Can I Keep Him?
LIMITED EDITION OF 2,500

COMMENTS: Issued 1994, *Original Retail:* $13.00

This piece sold out in 1995. This is the definition of "Charming." The motion in this piece makes you see poor Mackenzie trying to pack this little chick home for a new friend. It is as fabulous in person as it is pictured!

Sec. Mkt.: $315 - 350

_____ Have   _____ Want   _____ Paid

89604   Mackenzie Growing Beans
RETIRED 1995

COMMENTS: Issued 1995, *Original Retail:* $15.00

The seed packet pieces are darling displayed together. Mackenzie is one of the easiest to find.

Sec. Mkt.: $43 - 50

_____ Have   _____ Want   _____ Paid

Easter/Spring

89605 Binkey Growing Carrots ☐
RETIRED 1995

COMMENTS: Issued 1995, *Original Retail:* $15.00

Binkey peers over the top of the seed packet; a very heavy piece.

Sec. Mkt.: $50 - 60

_____ Have   _____ Want   _____ Paid

89606 Butterfly Smells Zinnia ☐
RETIRED 1995

COMMENTS: Issued 1994, *Original Retail:* $15.00

The hardest to find of the seed packets.

Sec. Mkt.: $65 - 75

_____ Have   _____ Want   _____ Paid

89607 Chauncey's Growing Tomatoes ☐
RETIRED 1995

COMMENTS: Issued 1995, *Original Retail:* $15.00

Top heavy; you might want to display them against a wall.

Sec. Mkt.: $40 - 50

_____ Have   _____ Want   _____ Paid

89609 Bunny Imposter ☐

COMMENTS: Issued 1996, *Original Retail:* $13.00

Mackenzie pretends to be a bunny. The leaves in his headband are fabric. Very fragile.

Sec. Mkt.: $18

_____ Have   _____ Want   _____ Paid

89615 Easter Parade ☐
RETIRED 1996

COMMENTS: Issued 1995, *Original Retail:* $10.00

Mackenzie is hanging from a balloon string in this Easter ornament. Originally packaged in cellophane.

Sec. Mkt.: $22 - 28

_____ Have   _____ Want   _____ Paid

Easter/Spring

89752 Binkey In Berry Patch
RETIRED 1996

COMMENTS: Issued 1995, *Original Retail:* $12.00

The strawberry on this hanging ornament looks good enough to eat!

Sec. Mkt.: $26 - 30

_____ Have   _____ Want   _____ Pa

89753 Peek-A-Boo
RETIRED 1996

COMMENTS: Issued 1995, *Original Retail:* $12.00

This is a darling Binkey piece, and still very affordable.

Sec. Mkt.: $28 - 35

_____ Have   _____ Want   _____ Paid

89754 Thanks For Being There
RETIRED 1996

COMMENTS: Issued 1996, *Original Retail:* $15.00

A good companion piece for *Life's A Picnic*. It is also in a music box from San Francisco Music Box Company. Found in a pale or "Naked" version.

Sec. Mkt.: $45 - 50

_____ Have   _____ Want   _____ Paid

98417 Feeding Time
RETIRED 1996

COMMENTS: Issued 1996, *Original Retail:* $16.00

Mackenzie is helping feed these babies. It is a lovely companion piece to *Slumber Party*. The birds are great on these pieces! Hopefully, there will be more of them in the line.

Sec. Mkt.: $45 - 60

_____ Have   _____ Want   _____ Paid

Lazy Days

83700   Toasting Marshmallows
COMMENTS: Issued 1998, *Original Retail:* $20.00

Binkey and Chauncey are toasting marshmallows over a burning campfire.

Sec. Mkt.: NE

_____ Have   _____ Want   _____ Paid

83701   Life's A Picnic With You
COMMENTS: Issued 1997, *Original Retail:* $18.00

What a great piece for an anniversary!

Sec. Mkt.: NE

_____ Have   _____ Want   _____ Paid

83702   Gone Fishin'
COMMENTS: Issued 1997, *Original Retail:* $16.00

Look at the fish on the back of this piece!

Sec. Mkt.: NE

_____ Have   _____ Want   _____ Paid

83703   Camping Out
COMMENTS: Issued 1998, *Original Retail:* $18.50

Mouse in a leaf tent, Lydia on head, acorn beside the tent. Great gift for the outdoor enthusiast!

Sec. Mkt.: NE

_____ Have   _____ Want   _____ Paid

Lazy Days

83704   The Blossom Bounce ☐

COMMENTS: Issued 1997, *Original Retail:* $20.00

Mackenzie is bouncing on the flower trampoline with a small wire.

Sec. Mkt.: NE

_____ Have   _____ Want   _____ Paid

83801   Row Boat Romance ☐

COMMENTS: Issued 1997, *Original Retail:* $13.50

This piece *Row Boat Romance* is seen in the 1997 catalog with a pink parasol. The issued piece was done with a white parasol. However, there are some pink parasols that escaped the factory. Be on the look out for them.

Sec. Mkt.: NE

_____ Have   _____ Want   _____ Paid

83802   Building Castles ☐

COMMENTS: Issued 1997, *Original Retail:* $17.00

The sand on this one is excellent. Haven't we all built sandcastles?

Sec. Mkt.: NE

_____ Have   _____ Want   _____ Paid

83803   A Day At The Lake ☐

COMMENTS: Issued 1998, *Original Retail:* $18.50

Binkey in a walnut boat, pulling a water skiing Mackenzie.

Sec. Mkt.: NE

_____ Have   _____ Want   _____ Paid

Lazy Days

83804   Come On In The Water's Fine ☐

COMMENTS: Issued 1998, *Original Retail:* $18.00

Binkey is sporting a life raft with scuba mask on top of his head. The snail is looking on.

Sec. Mkt.: NE

_____ Have   _____ Want   _____ Paid

83805   Stewart's Day In The Sun ☐

COMMENTS: Issued 1998, *Original Retail:* $17.00

Stewart is laying out in the sun. Looks like he should have used the sunscreen sooner! Some of these have been coming without the pink tummy.

Sec. Mkt.: NE

_____ Have   _____ Want   _____ Paid

Subscribe to the *Collectors' Bulletin*™

The Collectors' Bulletin™ has combined with Precious Collectibles®, The Ornament Collector™ and The Beanie Gazette™ to form one big information packed magazine!

6 Issues a Year
$23.95

6 issues a year

Learn the latest news on
Charming Tails™,
Boyds Bears™,
Hallmark Ornaments,
Precious Moments® Collectibles, Radko Ornaments, Polonaise Ornaments, Barbie and many more Collectibles!

Call or write to order
1-800-445-8745

Rosie Wells Enterprises, Inc.
22341 E. Wells Road, Dept. G.
Canton, IL 61520

Visit our website at
http://www.RosieWells.com

Call Now!
"Payment must be included with order."

The Wedding

82100 Here Comes The Bride

COMMENTS: Issued 1998, *Original Retail:* $17.00

Maxine has a beautiful leaf veil, complete with head piece and bridal bouquet, being carried by a couple of butterflies. The butterflies are different colors in the catalog.

Sec. Mkt.: NE

_____ Have   _____ Want   _____ Paid

82101 My Heart's All A Flutter (Groom)

COMMENTS: Issued 1998, *Original Retail:* $17.00

Mackenzie in a bow tie with hearts on wires. Very cute! Mackenzie and Maxine had their reception in Edison, New Jersey, April, 1998.

Sec. Mkt.: NE

_____ Have   _____ Want   _____ Paid

82102 Maid Of Honor

COMMENTS: Issued 1998, *Original Retail:* $16.00

Butterfly on wire; Lydia on Bunny's tail.

Sec. Mkt.: NE

_____ Have   _____ Want   _____ Paid

82103 The Best Bunny

COMMENTS: Issued 1998, *Original Retail:* $16.00

Bunny looks very dapper in a bow tie.

Sec. Mkt.: NE

_____ Have   _____ Want   _____ Paid

The Wedding

82104 The Ring Bearer ☐

COMMENTS: Issued 1998, *Original Retail:* $16.00

Stewart is carrying a ring pillow, complete with ring. Very darling! Oh, to be a Charming Tails collector planning a wedding this year! His hair is parted in the middle.

Sec. Mkt.: NE

_____ Have   _____ Want   _____ Paid

82105 Wedding Day Blossoms ☐

COMMENTS: Issued 1998, *Original Retail:* $16.00

A chipmunk throwing flowers, complete with flower bucket.

Sec. Mkt.: NE

_____ Have   _____ Want   _____ Paid

82107 The Get Away Car ☐

COMMENTS: Issued 1998, *Original Retail:* $22.00

This piece proved to be too small for a production mark. Collectors seem to have been very pleased with this one.

Sec. Mkt.: $25

_____ Have   _____ Want   _____ Paid

82108 The Altar Of Love ☐

COMMENTS: Issued 1998, *Original Retail:* $25.00

Reginald is taking the job as minister of the wedding. He is standing under an arched branch, love banner hanging above with the help of a couple of butterflies, complete with acorn bell.

Sec. Mkt.: NE

_____ Have   _____ Want   _____ Paid

The Wedding

82109 Together Forever

COMMENTS: Issued 1998, *Original Retail:* $25.00

Mackenzie and Maxine tangled in a heart, holding paws; grass under the heart. Cake topper with a milk white base; no understamp. Non-collectors have been drawn to this piece.

Sec. Mkt.: $35

_____ Have   _____ Want   _____ Paid

Only, the Squashville Gang had personal invitations to the big wedding. However, club members and guest at Eddison, New Jersey on April 18th and 19th, 1998, were invited to the reception honoring the larger than life couple, hosted by Fitz and Floyd.

85508 Open Pumpkin
RETIRED 1994

COMMENTS: Issued 1994, *Original Retail:* $15.00

This piece has a music disc in it that is light sensitive. When you open it, it plays "It's A Small World After All." Believe me, if you have this piece you know it plays, because it tends to go off whenever you turn on a light. Some have turned up without the music disc. I wonder if it was just more than some retailers could take? Also found in a pale version.

Sec. Mkt.: $60 - 75

_____ Have _____ Want _____ Paid

85510 Pumpkin Votive
RETIRED 1994

COMMENTS: Issued 1994, *Original Retail:* $13.50

This is really, really cute! I suspect even non-collectors of Charming Tails liked it. It is a little hard to find.

Sec. Mkt.: $45 - 60

_____ Have _____ Want _____ Paid

85512 Jumpin' Jack-O-Lanterns
RETIRED 1997

COMMENTS: Issued 1994, *Original Retail:* $17.00

Jumpin' Jack-O-Lanterns is already becoming difficult to find. Found in earlier catalogs as *Rabbit In Pumpkin.*

Sec. Mkt.: $29 - 35

_____ Have _____ Want _____ Paid

Tricks & Treats/Autumn Harvest

85607   Candy Corn Vampire
RETIRED 1996

COMMENTS: Issued 1995, *Original Retail:* $19.00

This is one of the most popular fall pieces.

Sec. Mkt.: $41 - 45

_____ Have   _____ Want   _____Paid

85611   Candy Apples
RETIRED 1996

COMMENTS: Issued 1995, *Original Retail:* $17.00

Mackenzie is decorating his apple for Halloween.

Sec. Mkt.: $25 - 30

_____ Have   _____ Want   _____Paid

85700   Stewart's Apple Costume

COMMENTS: Issued 1997, *Original Retail:* $12.50

Since the pieces are hand painted, you'll find some differences in painting. It is becoming more consistent.

Sec. Mkt.: NE

_____ Have   _____ Want   _____Paid

85701   Reginald's Gourd Costume

COMMENTS: Issued 1997, *Original Retail:* $12.50

This piece is one you need to see to appreciate; it is much sweeter in person.

Sec. Mkt.: NE

_____ Have   _____ Want   _____Paid

85703   Ghost Stories

COMMENTS: Issued 1997, *Original Retail:* $18.50

Do you see the owl in the tree? He is great! Think we might see more of him in the future? I certainly hope so!

Sec. Mkt.: $20

_____ Have   _____ Want   _____Paid

Tricks & Treats/Autumn Harvest

85704   The Good Witch

COMMENTS: Issued 1997, *Original Retail:* $18.50

This piece is becoming difficult to locate, but it is still out there at retail. It just might take some work to find it.

Sec. Mkt.: $20

_____ Have   _____ Want   _____ Paid

87428   Look! No Hands

COMMENTS: Issued 1996, *Original Retail:* $16.50

Mackenzie seems quite adept at juggling candy corn. The wire was bent on some, but it can usually be straightened gently.

Sec. Mkt.: NE

_____ Have   _____ Want   _____ Paid

87429   Binkey's Acorn Costume

COMMENTS: Issued 1996, *Original Retail:* $12.50

Binkey looks to be inquisitive in this piece.

Sec. Mkt.: NE

_____ Have   _____ Want   _____ Paid

87430   Maxine's Pumpkin Costume

COMMENTS: Issued 1995, *Original Retail:* $13.00

Maxine is quite charming in her pumpkin outfit, all ready for trick or treat. She is difficult to find.

Sec. Mkt.: $18

_____ Have   _____ Want   _____ Paid

87431   Chauncey's Pear Costume

COMMENTS: Issued 1996, *Original Retail:* $13.00

The Squashville Gang seems to be ready for Halloween in their fruit and vegetable costumes. They look great all grouped together.

Sec. Mkt.: NE

_____ Have   _____ Want   _____ Paid

Tricks & Treats/Autumn Harvest

87436   Bag Of Tricks... Or Treats ☐
COMMENTS: Issued 1996, *Original Retail:* $16.50

The candy corn and the candy pumpkins look real. Look for this piece to retire soon.

Sec. Mkt.: $20

_____ Have   _____ Want   _____ Paid

87440   You're Not Scary ☐
COMMENTS: Issued 1996, *Original Retail:* $15.00

This is a great piece, quite adorable!

Sec. Mkt.: $25 - 30

_____ Have   _____ Want   _____ Paid

Read The
Weekly Collectors' Gazette™

Featuring the most up-to-date news on:
Charming Tails™,
Precious Moments® Collectibles, Boyds™, Cherished Teddies®, Beanie Babies™ and More!

Secondary Market Price Updates and More!
By subscription, this weekly publication is only $2 an issue, 8 week minimum.

Call Now!

You'll Hear It Here First!

1-800-445-8745

34

Giving Thanks

85398 Gourd Slide
RETIRED 1996

COMMENTS: Issued 1994, *Original Retail*: $16.00

This is really cute displayed with *Pumpkin Slide*. Also found in a pale version. Found in earlier catalogs as *Mouse On Gourd Slide*.

Sec. Mkt.: $35 - 50

_____ Have   _____ Want   _____ Paid

85399 Cornfield Feast
RETIRED 1994

COMMENTS: Issued 1994, *Original Retail*: $15.00

There are two different variations. The mice aren't antiqued in one variation, and appear to be more flesh toned than gray. It was a factory painting error. Also found in a pale version. Found in earlier catalogs as *Mice On Corn*.

Sec. Mkt.: $85 - 100

_____ Have   _____ Want   _____ Paid

85400 Mouse Pumpkin Candleholder/ Facing Away
RETIRED 1995

COMMENTS: Issued 1994, *Original Retail*: $13.00 ea.

There are two different styles with the same item number. In one, the mouse faces the candle. In the other, the mouse faces away from the candle. This is a light colored mouse notice the difference.

Sec. Mkt.: $90 - 125

_____ Have   _____ Want   _____ Paid

Giving Thanks/Autumn Harvest

85400 Mouse Pumpkin Candleholder/ Facing
RETIRED 1994

COMMENTS: Issued 1994, *Original Retail:* $15.00

There are two different styles with the same item number. In one, the mouse faces the candle. In the other, the mouse faces away from the candle. Also found in a pale version.

Sec. Mkt.: $90 - 125

_____ Have   _____ Want   _____ Paid

85401 Fall Frolicking/ Under a Mushroom
RETIRED 1996

COMMENTS: Issued 1994, *Original Retail:* $13.00

Two styles with the same item number. These two little mice are becoming one of the most difficult to find in the collection. Variations in coloring of the mice can be found. Watch for the price to escalate in the future. Found in earlier catalogs as *Mice With Leaves Ornament.*

Sec. Mkt.: $45 - 75

_____ Have   _____ Want   _____ Paid

85401 Fall Frolicking/Under a Leaf
RETIRED 1996

COMMENTS: Issued 1994, *Original Retail:* $13.00

Two styles with the same item number. These two little mice are becoming one of the most difficult to find in the collection. This can be found with light colored mice. Watch for the price to escalate in the future.

Sec. Mkt.: $45 - 75

_____ Have   _____ Want   _____ Paid

85402 Caps Off To You
RETIRED 1996

COMMENTS: Issued 1994, *Original Retail:* $10.00

This looks great with *Acorn Built For Two*. Variations in coloring of the mice can be found. Found in earlier catalogs as *Mouse In Acorn.*

Sec. Mkt.: $25 - 35

_____ Have   _____ Want   _____ Paid

Giving Thanks/Autumn Harvest

85403 Acorn Built For Two
RETIRED 1996

COMMENTS: Issued 1993, *Original Retail:* $11.50

This is a very inexpensive piece and Mackenzie and Maxine look very sweet sharing an acorn. This can be found with light colored mice. Found in earlier catalogs as *Mouse In Acorn*.

Sec. Mkt.: $35 - 50

_____ Have   _____ Want   _____ Paid

85410 Jack O' Lantern Jalopy
COMMENTS: Issued 1998, *Original Retail:* $18.00

Reginald is driving a pumpkin carriage, complete with nut slice wheels and steering wheel.

Sec. Mkt.: NE

_____ Have   _____ Want   _____ Paid

85411 Pumpkin's First Pumpkin
COMMENTS: Issued 1998, *Original Retail:* $17.00

Bunny is carrying a pumpkin with a baby bunny holding a pumpkin behind her and leaves on the ground.

Sec. Mkt.: NE

_____ Have   _____ Want   _____ Paid

85412 Turkey With Dressing
COMMENTS: Issued 1998, *Original Retail:* $18.00

Binkey is dressing a real turkey with a beautiful bow. I love this one!

Sec. Mkt.: NE

_____ Have   _____ Want   _____ Paid

Giving Thanks/Autumn Harvest

85416   Stack O' Lanterns

COMMENTS: Issued 1998, *Original Retail:* $18.00

Mackenzie is standing on a Jack O' Lantern, with one behind him, building a stack of Jack O' Lanterns five high. This piece looks great!

Sec. Mkt.: NE

_____ Have   _____ Want   _____ Paid

85417   Booo!

COMMENTS: Issued 1998, *Original Retail:* $18.00

Binkey is being frightened by a masked Mackenzie standing behind a pumpkin; candy corn on the ground.

Sec. Mkt.: NE

_____ Have   _____ Want   _____ Paid

85507   Harvest Fruit/Binkey
RETIRED 1995

COMMENTS: Issued 1994, *Original Retail:* $16.00

The pins that hinge the two pieces (same item number) come apart easily.

Sec. Mkt.: $45 - 60

_____ Have   _____ Want   _____ Paid

85507   Harvest Fruit/Chauncey
RETIRED 1995

COMMENTS: Issued 1994, *Original Retail:* $16.00

The pins that hinge the two pieces (same item number) come apart easily.

Sec. Mkt.: $45 - 60

_____ Have   _____ Want   _____ Paid

85509   Pear Candleholder
RETIRED 1994

COMMENTS: Issued 1994, *Original Retail:* $14.00

There is only one style of the pear candleholder with the mouse facing the candle. Also found in a pale version.

Sec. Mkt.: $65 - 90

_____ Have   _____ Want   _____ Paid

Giving Thanks/Autumn Harvest

85511 Frosting Pumpkins
RETIRED 1996

COMMENTS: Issued 1994, *Original Retail:* $16.00

Now you know who is responsible for putting the frost on the pumpkins every year! Found in a pale or "Naked" version.

Sec. Mkt.: $37 - 50

_____ Have   _____ Want   _____ Paid

85513 Pumpkin Slide
RETIRED 1995

COMMENTS: Issued 1994, *Original Retail:* $16.00

A great companion piece for *Gourd Slide.* Also found in a pale version. Found in earlier catalogs as *Mouse Slide.*

Sec. Mkt.: $35 - 45

_____ Have   _____ Want   _____ Paid

85514 Painting Leaves
RETIRED 1996

COMMENTS: Issued 1994, *Original Retail:* $16.00

A great companion piece for *Oops I Missed*! Found in earlier catalogs as *Mouse Painting Leaves.*

Sec. Mkt.: $35 - 40

_____ Have   _____ Want   _____ Paid

85516 Stump Candleholder/ Beside Candleholder
RETIRED 1994

COMMENTS: Issued 1994, *Original Retail:* $20.00

Two of the hardest pieces to find in the collection. Again, two designs, one item number. One mouse is beside the stump and the other mouse is behind the leaves. Found in a pale or "Naked" version.

Sec. Mkt.: $85 - 100

_____ Have   _____ Want   _____ Paid

Giving Thanks/Autumn Harvest

85516 Stump Candleholder/ Behind Leaf
RETIRED 1994

COMMENTS: Issued 1994, *Original Retail:* $20.00

Two of the hardest pieces to find in the collection. Again, two designs, one item number. One mouse is beside the stump and the other mouse is behind the leaves. Also found in a pale version.

Sec. Mkt.: $85 - 100

_____ Have _____ Want _____ Paid

85606 Pumpkin Pie
RETIRED 1996

COMMENTS: Issued 1995, *Original Retail:* $16.00

The pie has appeared with both yellow and orange pie filling the yellow being the older. Neither is more valuable at this time. A few have been seen with white pie filling. Also found in a pale version.

Sec. Mkt.: $35 - 45

_____ Have _____ Want _____ Paid

85608 Giving Thanks
RETIRED 1996

COMMENTS: Issued 1995, *Original Retail:* $17.00

Mackenzie and Binkey say grace over their wonderful bounty.

Sec. Mkt.: $25 - 40

_____ Have _____ Want _____ Paid

85610 Horn Of Plenty
RETIRED 1996

COMMENTS: Issued 1995, *Original Retail:* $21.00

This is a fabulous piece! It will look great on any Thanksgiving table.

Sec. Mkt.: $30 - 40

_____ Have _____ Want _____ Paid

Giving Thanks/Autumn Harvest

85615 Garden Naptime
RETIRED 1997
COMMENTS: Issued 1995, *Original Retail:* $19.00

Mackenzie and the snail are nose to nose; so wonderful!

Sec. Mkt.: $25 - 30

_____ Have   _____ Want   _____ Paid

85702 Turkey Traveller
COMMENTS: Issued 1997, *Original Retail:* $18.50

The gourd turkey is wonderful; leaves make the feathers. A collector's favorite, this turkey is hard to find.

Sec. Mkt.: $20

_____ Have   _____ Want   _____ Paid

85776 Let's Get Crackin'
RETIRED 1997
COMMENTS: Issued 1995, *Original Retail:* $21.00

Until the new packaging began, a lot arrived broken.

Sec. Mkt.: $35 - 45

_____ Have   _____ Want   _____ Paid

85777 Reginald's Hideaway
RETIRED 1996
COMMENTS: Issued 1995, *Original Retail:* $14.00

Reginald is fast becoming to be a hit with Charming Tails fans. The men seem to like him.

Sec. Mkt.: $45 - 50

_____ Have   _____ Want   _____ Paid

Giving Thanks/Autumn Harvest

87044 Mouse With Apple Candleholder/ Facing Away from Candle
RETIRED 1995

COMMENTS: Issued 1993, *Original Retail:* $13.00

One mouse faces the candle and is awake while the other mouse faces away from the candle and is asleep. Also found in light and dark mice.

Sec. Mkt.: $70 - 95

_____ Have   _____ Want   _____ Paid

87044 Mouse With Apple Candleholder/ Facing Candle
RETIRED 1995

COMMENTS: Issued 1993, *Original Retail:* $13.00

Two styles, same item number. One mouse faces the candle and is awake while the other mouse faces away from the candle and is asleep. Also found in light and dark mice.

Sec. Mkt.: $70 - 95

_____ Have   _____ Want   _____ Paid

87438 Pickin' Time
RETIRED 1997

COMMENTS: Issued 1996, *Original Retail:* $17.00

Lydia and the snail are helping Reginald with his harvest.

Sec. Mkt.: $20 - 25

_____ Have   _____ Want   _____ Paid

87443 Oops! I Missed

COMMENTS: Issued 1996, *Original Retail:* $17.00

A great companion piece for *Painting Leaves*.

Sec. Mkt.: NE

_____ Have   _____ Want   _____ Paid

Giving Thanks/Autumn Harvest

87445 Pilgrim's Progress

COMMENTS: Issued 1996, *Original Retail:* $14.50

Can you think of any other piece in which has Mackenzie with a leaf collar?

Sec. Mkt.: NE

_____ Have   _____ Want   _____ Paid

87446 Indian Imposter

COMMENTS: Issued 1996, *Original Retail:* $15.00

Binkey is pretending to be an Indian. Catalog shows a different ribbon.

Sec. Mkt.: NE

_____ Have   _____ Want   _____ Paid

87451 You're Nutty

COMMENTS: Issued 1996, *Original Retail:* $13.00

Chauncey seems to be storing nuts for the winter. The top acorn is attached by a spring.

Sec. Mkt.: NE

_____ Have   _____ Want   _____ Paid

Christmas Parade

87473 Follow In My Footsteps

COMMENTS: Issued 1996, *Original Retail:* $13.00
The little mouse will have a hard time filling Mackenzie's footprints in the hearts of collectors! This is one of the most endearing pieces.

Sec. Mkt.: $25

_____ Have _____ Want _____ Paid

87543 Parade Banner

COMMENTS: Issued 1996, *Original Retail:* $17.00
Binkey and Mackenzie start off the parade.

Sec. Mkt.: NE

_____ Have _____ Want _____ Paid

87554 Chauncey's Noisemakers

COMMENTS: Issued 1996, *Original Retail:* $13.00
Line up the parade on your mantle, add a little fake snow and it will make a wonderful scene!

Sec. Mkt.: NE

_____ Have _____ Want _____ Paid

87555 Holiday Trumpeter

COMMENTS: Issued 1996, *Original Retail:* $13.00
This bunny plays a mean trumpet, but doesn't seem to be bothering the *Drummer Mouse* in the 1997 Catalog; an error in the display page.

Sec. Mkt.: NE

_____ Have _____ Want _____ Paid

Christmas Parade/Squashville

87556 The Drum Major ☐
COMMENTS: Issued 1996, *Original Retail:* $13.00
Reginald's baton is broken easily; handle with care.
Sec. Mkt.: NE

_____ Have _____ Want _____ Paid

87557 Little Drummer Boy ☐
COMMENTS: Issued 1996, *Original Retail:* $13.00
Stewart and Mackenzie are always getting confused when talking about the *Drummer Mouse* and the *Drummer Boy*. It's easy to figure out. Just remember, Mackenzie is the mouse and Stewart is the boy!
Sec. Mkt.: NE

_____ Have _____ Want _____ Paid

87575 Christmas Stroll ☐
COMMENTS: Issued 1996, *Original Retail:* $17.00
Bunny is walking baby in the stroller to see the parade.
Sec. Mkt.: NE

_____ Have _____ Want _____ Paid

87587 The Float Driver ☐
COMMENTS: Issued 1996, *Original Retail:* $13.00
Companion piece for *Mackenzie Claus*.
Sec. Mkt.: NE

_____ Have _____ Want _____ Paid

Christmas Parade/Squashville

87696   Town Crier

COMMENTS: Issued 1996, *Original Retail:* $15.00

In the tradition of Old English Town Criers, Binkey announces the parade.

Sec. Mkt.: NE

_____ Have   _____ Want   _____ Paid

87708   The Santa Balloon

COMMENTS: Issued 1997, *Original Retail:* $25.00

One of the neatest pieces! Santa is suspended on wires.

Sec. Mkt.: NE

_____ Have   _____ Want   _____ Paid

87713   Christmas Trio

COMMENTS: Issued 1997, *Original Retail:* $15.50

The Squashville gang begins to go caroling.

Sec. Mkt.: NE

_____ Have   _____ Want   _____ Paid

Austin Hauk poses with his auntie's Charming Tails.

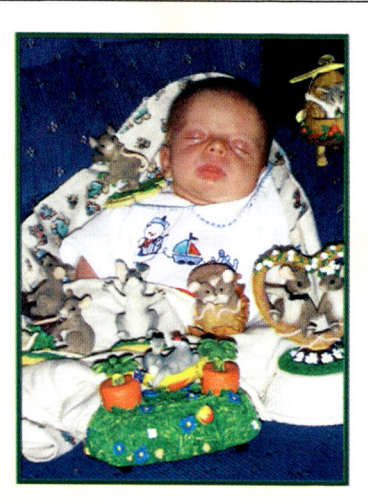

Deck The Halls

86652   Air Mail To Santa ☐
COMMENTS: Issued 1998, *Original Retail:* $13.00

Mackenzie riding a letter, waving.

Sec. Mkt.: NE

_____ Have   _____ Want   _____ Paid

86653   Our First Christmas Together ☐
Third Edition
COMMENTS: Issued 1998, *Original Retail:* $13.00

Mackenzie and Maxine in a peanut. This is limited to year of production.

Sec. Mkt.: NE

_____ Have   _____ Want   _____ Paid

86655   Bundle Of Joy ☐
COMMENTS: Issued 1998, *Original Retail:* $13.00

A Chickadee carrying a mouse in a banner bearing the inscription "First Christmas."

Sec. Mkt.: NE

_____ Have   _____ Want   _____ Paid

86656   Heading For The Slopes ☐
COMMENTS: Issued 1998, *Original Retail:* $13.00

Binkey on skis, trying to hop on chair lift.

Sec. Mkt.: NE

_____ Have   _____ Want   _____ Paid

Deck the Halls/Squashville

86657   Ski Jumper   ☐
COMMENTS: Issued 1998, *Original Retail:* $13.00
Binkey riding a ski lift, complete with ski poles.
Sec. Mkt.: NE

_____ Have   _____ Want   _____ Paid

86658   Tricycle Built From Treats   ☐
COMMENTS: Issued 1998, *Original Retail:* $13.00
Reginald is riding a peppermint tricycle.
Sec. Mkt.: NE

_____ Have   _____ Want   _____ Paid

86659   Pine Cone Predicament   ☐
1998 ANNUAL, DATED
COMMENTS: Issued 1998, *Original Retail:* $13.00

Mackenzie in a branch with pine cones; looks very different from other Charming Tails. Limited edition by year.
Sec. Mkt.: NE

_____ Have   _____ Want   _____ Paid

86660   All Lit Up/Lighted Ornament   ☐
COMMENTS: Issued 1997, *Original Retail:* $11.00
Difficult to find.
Sec. Mkt.: NE

_____ Have   _____ Want   _____ Paid

86701   Maxine's Angel   ☐
COMMENTS: Issued 1997, *Original Retail:* $9.00
Would look good with the Nativity.
Sec. Mkt.: NE

_____ Have   _____ Want   _____ Paid

Deck the Halls/Squashville

86704 Mackenzie In A Mitten ☐
RETIRED 1997
COMMENTS: Issued 1997, *Original Retail:* $9.00
Already a little harder to find.
Sec. Mkt.: $16 - 18

_____ Have _____ Want _____ Paid

86707 A Special Delivery ☐
COMMENTS: Issued 1997, *Original Retail:* $9.00
A clever gift if you have a secret pal.
Sec. Mkt.: NE

_____ Have _____ Want _____ Paid

86708 Our First Christmas ☐
RETIRED 1997
COMMENTS: Issued 1997, *Original Retail:* $12.50
Limited to year of production, not numbered. Wouldn't it be a fun way to add mistletoe to your doorway? Careful where you stand!
Sec. Mkt.: $14 - 18

_____ Have _____ Want _____ Paid

86709 Mackenzie's Jack In The Box ☐
RETIRED 1997
COMMENTS: Issued 1997, *Original Retail:* $10.00
Limited to 1997; was retired at the end of the year. Very popular with collectors; also dated. I think this is one to watch in the future.
Sec. Mkt.: $15 - 20

_____ Have _____ Want _____ Paid

86710 Chauncey's First Christmas ☐
RETIRED 1997
COMMENTS: Issued 1997, *Original Retail:* $9.00
Our favorite chipmunk Chauncey is depicted as a baby chipmunk, complete with diapers. What a wonderful baby's first Christmas.
Sec. Mkt.: $15 - 18

_____ Have _____ Want _____ Paid

Deck the Halls/Squashville

86784 The Drifters
RETIRED 1997

COMMENTS: Issued 1991, *Original Retail:* $12.00

One of the **Original 12** designs we have come to love as Charming Tails. These can be found with the variation of light colored mice.

Sec. Mkt.: $31 - 38

_____ Have   _____ Want   _____ Paid

86784 The Drifters
RETIRED 1997

COMMENTS: Issued 1993, *Original Retail:* $12.00

One of the **Original 12.** These pieces share the same item number. This li'l mouse is so cute parachuting with a leaf. Variations in lightness or darkness of coloring on the mouse can be found. Found in earlier catalogs as *Drifters*.

Sec. Mkt.: $31 - 38

_____ Have   _____ Want   _____ Paid

86785 Catching ZZZ's
RETIRED 1995

COMMENTS: Issued 1991, *Original Retail:* $12.00

One of the **Original 12.** The Chickadee was first named as *Belle*. The piece is shown in a catalog, *Belle and Maxine Catchin' ZZZ's*. Variations in lightness or darkness of coloring on the mouse can be found. Found in earlier catalogs as *Mouse And Bird On Leaf Ornament*.

Sec. Mkt.: $28 - 35

_____ Have   _____ Want   _____ Paid

86786 Mice In Leaf Sleigh
RETIRED 1995

COMMENTS: Issued 1992, *Original Retail:* $26.00

One of the **Original 12.** In searching for this piece, I was told by one retailer that she had them so long, she sold them for $2 each! Wish I'd been there! It is very difficult to find. Variations of colored mice can be found.

Sec. Mkt.: $250 - 275

_____ Have   _____ Want   _____ Paid

Deck the Halls/Squashville

86787 Chickadees On Ball
RETIRED 1995

COMMENTS: Issued 1992, *Original Retail:* $13.50

One of the **Original 12**. They are probably out there on the trees of bird collectors, or people who have no idea what Charming Tails are.

Sec. Mkt.: $125 - 175

_____ Have   _____ Want   _____ Paid

86788 Rabbit On Glass Ball/Holly
RETIRED 1995

COMMENTS: Issued 1992, *Original Retail:* $12.00

One of the **Original 12**. Wonderful pieces sharing the same item number. .

Sec. Mkt.: $48 - 60

_____ Have   _____ Want   _____ Paid

86788 Mouse On Glass Ball/Holly
RETIRED 1995

COMMENTS: Issued 1992, *Original Retail:* $12.00

One of the **Original 12.** Also found in a pale version

Sec. Mkt.: $43 - 55

_____ Have   _____ Want   _____ Paid

86789 Fresh Fruit/Binkey
RETIRED 1995

COMMENTS: Issued 1992, *Original Retail:* $12.00

One of the **Original 12**. Binkey is in the apple. There are three with the same item number. Dean Griff was raised near an orchard. Found in earlier catalogs as *Animals In Fruit*.

Sec. Mkt.: $25 - 30

_____ Have   _____ Want   _____ Paid

86789 Fresh Fruit/Mackenzie
RETIRED 1995

COMMENTS: Issued 1992, *Original Retail:* $12.00

One of the **Original 12**. Found in earlier catalogs as *Animals In Fruit*.

Sec. Mkt.: $25 - 50

_____ Have   _____ Want   _____ Paid

Deck the Halls/Squashville

86789 Fresh Fruit/Belle
RETIRED 1995

COMMENTS: Issued 1991, *Original Retail:* $12.00

One of the **Original 12.** Found in the 1993 catalog as "Dean Griff Woodland Collection," this was earlier introduced with 11 others in the Silvestri's 1991 catalog. They did so well, Dean was commissioned to do more.

Sec. Mkt.: $25 - 30

_____ Have   _____ Want   _____ Paid

86791 Chicks w/Bead Garland
RETIRED 1995

COMMENTS: Issued 1991, *Original Retail:* $17.50

One of the **Original 12.** These two little birds have very fragile beaks and hold a few strands of little wooden beads. They clip onto a branch. Very difficult piece to add to your collection.

Sec. Mkt.: $65 - 90

_____ Have   _____ Want   _____ Paid

87027 Pear House/Lighted
RETIRED 1995

COMMENTS: Issued 1994, *Original Retail:* $13.00
Very small ($3^{1}/_{2}$").

Sec. Mkt.: $45 - 50

_____ Have   _____ Want   _____ Paid

87032 Apple House/Lighted
RETIRED 1995

COMMENTS: Issued 1994, *Original Retail:* $13.00

Small, $3^{1}/_{2}$" tall. This is a great alternative to the big house pieces until you expand your collection.

Sec. Mkt.: $47 - 50

_____ Have   _____ Want   _____ Paid

Deck the Halls/Squashville

87036 Porcelain Mouse Bell
RETIRED 1995

COMMENTS: Issued 1993, *Original Retail:* $5.00

This mouse is the only one in the collection that seems to bear little resemblance to what we now know as Mackenzie. Very few of these have been sold.

Sec. Mkt.: $225 - 250

_____ Have   _____ Want   _____ Paid

87037 Mouse On Snowflake
RETIRED 1995

COMMENTS: Issued 1993, *Original Retail:* $11.00

Lighted snowflake; snow has yellowed on many. Also found in a pale version.

Sec. Mkt.: $32 - 40

_____ Have   _____ Want   _____ Paid

87038 Bunny Crystal Bell
RETIRED 1995

COMMENTS: Issued 1994, *Original Retail:* $10.50

The bunny is on top of the bell, the mouse is the clapper. Same item number, the mouse and bunny on the top are the same as on the glass ball, and the clappers look like the ones in the Holiday Wreath. Not enough of these have been sold to establish a firm price; the ones known in existence aren't for sale.

Sec. Mkt.: $350 - 375

_____ Have   _____ Want   _____ Paid

Remember - laughter is "internal jogging."

Deck the Halls/Squashville

87038 Mouse Crystal Bell
RETIRED *1995*

COMMENTS: Issued 1994, *Original Retail:* $10.50

There is a mouse on top of the bell and a mouse on the clapper. On the other bunny is the top of the bell and mouse is on clapper. Same item number, the mouse and bunny on the top are the same as on the glass ball, and the clappers look like the ones in the *Holiday Wreath*. Not enough of these have been sold to establish a firm price, the ones known in existence aren't for sale.

Sec. Mkt.: $350 - 375

_____ Have   _____ Want   _____ Paid

87045 Mouse On Yellow Bulb
RETIRED *1995*

COMMENTS: Issued 1995, *Original Retail:* $10.00

There is some rumor that this piece was issued as a GCC Exclusive.

Sec. Mkt.: $38 - 45

_____ Have   _____ Want   _____ Paid

87184 Baby's First Christmas
RETIRED *1994*

COMMENTS: Issued 1994, *Original Retail:* $12.00

Limited by year; hangs by a small chain.

Sec. Mkt.: $31 - 35

_____ Have   _____ Want   _____ Paid

Learn from yesterday

Live for today

Hope for tomorrow.

Deck the Halls/Squashville

87185 Maxine And Mackenzie
RETIRED 1996

COMMENTS: Issued 1994, *Original Retail:* $13.00

Not sure how to tell the difference. Two styles, same item number.

Sec. Mkt.: $27 - 35

_____ Have   _____ Want   _____ Paid

87185 Maxine & Mackenzie
RETIRED 1996

COMMENTS: Issued 1994, *Original Retail:* $13.00

Mouse hanging down on leaf. Two styles, same item number.

Sec. Mkt.: $27 - 35

_____ Have   _____ Want   _____ Paid

87186 The Grape Escape/Mackenzie
RETIRED 1995

COMMENTS: Issued 1994, *Original Retail:* $18.00

The grapes on these are fabulous! Two styles, same item number. Mackenzie on green grapes.

Sec. Mkt.: $45 - 55

_____ Have   _____ Want   _____ Paid

87186 The Grape Escape/Binkey
RETIRED 1995

COMMENTS: Issued 1994, *Original Retail:* $18.00

Two styles, same item number. Binkey on purple grapes.

Sec. Mkt.: $44 - 55

_____ Have   _____ Want   _____ Paid

Don't grumble because you don't have what you want - be thankful you don't get what you deserve.

Deck the Halls/Squashville

87187 Binkey's Snack
RETIRED 1994

COMMENTS: Issued 1994, *Original Retail:* $12.00

Two styles, same item number. Binkey on plums. Sometimes, he is hanging upside down. This said to be a factory error.

Sec. Mkt.: $59 - 65

_____ Have   _____ Want   _____ Paid

87187 Mackenzie's Snack
RETIRED 1994

COMMENTS: Issued 1994, *Original Retail:* $12.00

Two styles, same item number. Mackenzie is on the cherries.

Sec. Mkt.: $54 - 65

_____ Have   _____ Want   _____ Paid

87188 Lady Bug Express
RETIRED 1994

COMMENTS: Issued 1994, *Original Retail:* $18.00

This piece has a string to hang it, but is much too heavy to hang. It is one of the most sought after of the collection. The ladybug was named at The Flamingo Fling in 1996, and announced at the Florida Extravaganza in 1997. Her name is Lydia. Collectors, Candy Fierro and Doug Lowery, named her appropriately. Lydia has been seen with red and black antennae ends. Though not a limited edition, 7,500 were to be produced with and without registration numbers.

Sec. Mkt.: $175 - 200

_____ Have   _____ Want   _____ Paid

A candle loses nothing by lighting another candle.

Deck the Halls/Squashville

87189 Mouse Candle Climber
RETIRED 1995

COMMENTS: Issued 1994, *Original Retail:* $8.00

This little mouse's arms go around a taper. It looks wonderful with the *Mouse In A Treehole* candleholder. The mouse may be found in different variations, light or dark brown, but is typically a lighter grey.

Sec. Mkt.: $40 - 50

_____ Have _____ Want _____ Paid

87191 Mackenzie Blowing Bubbles
RETIRED 1994

COMMENTS: Issued 1994, *Original Retail:* $12.00

This is a hard one to find. I suppose it is because of its undeniable charm.

Sec. Mkt.: $55 - 60

_____ Have _____ Want _____ Paid

87192 Mackenzie Bubble Ride
RETIRED 1996

COMMENTS: Issued 1995, *Original Retail:* $13.00

Some of these were mistakenly numbered as limited edition. If you get to choose, go ahead and choose one with the numbers. At present time it doesn't make any difference in secondary market value.

Sec. Mkt.: $35 - 45

_____ Have _____ Want _____ Paid

87199 Reginald's Bubble Ride
RETIRED 1994

COMMENTS: Issued 1994, *Original Retail:* $12.00

Hard to find. Raccoon collectors have snatched him up, I'll bet. He was first listed as *Reginald's Great Adventure*.

Sec. Mkt.: $49 - 55

_____ Have _____ Want _____ Paid

Deck the Halls/Squashville

87202   Horsing Around
RETIRED 1996
COMMENTS: Issued 1994, *Original Retail:* $18.00
Mackenzie looks cute riding his hobby horse.
Sec. Mkt.: $30 - 35

_____ Have   _____ Want   _____ Paid

87299   Holiday Balloon Ride
RETIRED 1996
COMMENTS: Issued 1995, *Original Retail:* $16.00
The leaves make a ball-shaped balloon and the basket is attached with red ribbons.
Sec. Mkt.: $31 - 38

_____ Have   _____ Want   _____ Paid

87300   Mackenzie's Whirlygig
RETIRED 1997
COMMENTS: Issued 1995, *Original Retail:* $21.00
Notice Mackenzie waving.
Sec. Mkt.: $40 - 50

_____ Have   _____ Want   _____ Paid

87301   Christmas Cookies/Reginald
COMMENTS: Issued 1995, *Original Retail:* $11.00
Three different designs with the same number.
Sec. Mkt.: $18 - 25

_____ Have   _____ Want   _____ Paid

Deck the Halls/Squashville

87301   Christmas Cookies/Binkey ☐
COMMENTS: Issued 1995, *Original Retail:* $11.00
These look great with *Oops, Did I Do That?*
Sec. Mkt.: $18 - 25

_____ Have   _____ Want   _____ Paid

87301   Christmas Cookies/Mackenzie ☐
COMMENTS: Issued 1995, *Original Retail:* $11.00
At this time, no one design is more valuable. However, there are only mice collectors and bunny collectors. I even know a couple of raccoon collectors. So we will have to wait and see which one the collectors have a more difficult time finding.
Sec. Mkt.: $18 - 25

_____ Have   _____ Want   _____ Paid

87302   Reginald In Leaves/ ☐
Raccoon Parachuting
RETIRED 1997
COMMENTS: Issued 1995, *Original Retail:* $11.00
Overlooked for awhile; now becoming very difficult to find at retail.
Sec. Mkt.: $20 - 30

_____ Have   _____ Want   _____ Paid

87302   Reginald In Leaves/ ☐
Raccoon Riding Leaf
RETIRED 1997
COMMENTS: Issued 1995, *Original Retail:* $11.00
Also shares the same item number. Becoming very hard to find! You may have to trade or find an alternative to your regular retailer.
Sec. Mkt.: $18 - 25

_____ Have   _____ Want   _____ Paid

Deck the Halls/Squashville

87303 Binkey's Poinsettia
RETIRED 1997

COMMENTS: Issued 1995, *Original Retail:* $13.00

Sweet piece; seems to be catching on in popularity. Sold out in 1997.

Sec. Mkt.: $18 - 25

_____ Have   _____ Want   _____ Paid

87304 Christmas Flowers

COMMENTS: Issued 1995, *Original Retail:* $13.00

Wouldn't this look lovely in a display of poinsettias for a centerpiece?

Sec. Mkt.: $18

_____ Have   _____ Want   _____ Paid

87306 1995 Annual Ornament/Stocking
1995 LIMITED EDITION

COMMENTS: Issued 1995, *Original Retail:* $16.00

Sec. Mkt.: $26 - 30

_____ Have   _____ Want   _____ Paid

87307 Stewart's Winter Fun/Snowflake
RETIRED 1995

COMMENTS: Issued 1995, *Original Retail:* $10.00

Stewart is on an icicle and on a snowflake; both have the same item number. Found in earlier catalogs as *Skunk On Sled*.

Sec. Mkt.: $23 - 28

_____ Have   _____ Want   _____ Paid

Deck the Halls/Squashville

87307 Stewart's Winter Fun/Icicle
RETIRED 1995

COMMENTS: Issued 1995, *Original Retail:* $10.00

Stewart is on an icicle and on a snowflake; both have the same item number. Found in earlier catalogs as *Skunk On Icicle*.

Sec. Mkt.: $25 - 30

_____ Have   _____ Want   _____ Paid

87308 Stewart At Play
RETIRED 1995

COMMENTS: Issued 1995, *Original Retail:* $12.00

Adorable hanging on a fall display!

Sec. Mkt.: $23 - 28

_____ Have   _____ Want   _____ Paid

87314 Peppermint Party/Balancing Mint

COMMENTS: Issued 1995, *Original Retail:* $11.00

Two designs with same item number.

Sec. Mkt.: $18 - 25

_____ Have   _____ Want   _____ Paid

Deck the Halls/Squashville

87485 Christmas Stamps

COMMENTS: Issued 1996, *Original Retail:* $13.00

This is one you need to see in person to appreciate.

Sec. Mkt.: NE

_____ Have _____ Want _____ Paid

87486 Letter To Santa
RETIRED 1997

COMMENTS: Issued 1996, *Original Retail:* $13.00

Very heavy piece. Mackenzie seems to have gotten his tail caught under the stamps. Great detail!

Sec. Mkt.: $18 - 22

_____ Have _____ Want _____ Paid

87490 Flights Of Fancy
RETIRED 1997

COMMENTS: Issued 1996, *Original Retail:* $13.00

Cute addition to the Nativity.

Sec. Mkt.: $15 - 20

_____ Have _____ Want _____ Paid

87492 Frequent Flyer
RETIRED 1997

COMMENTS: Issued 1996, *Original Retail:* $13.00

Notice the gang has their halos on.

Sec. Mkt.: $15 - 20

_____ Have _____ Want _____ Paid

87492 Fallen Angel
RETIRED 1997

COMMENTS: Issued 1996, *Original Retail:* $13.00

It's hard to remember these piece names and which goes with which.

Sec. Mkt.: $15 - 20

_____ Have _____ Want _____ Paid

Deck the Halls/Squashville

87493 Weeeeeee!
RETIRED 1997
COMMENTS: Issued 1996, *Original Retail:* $13.00
A few of the Squashville Gang join the falling leaves in play.
Sec. Mkt.: $15 - 20

_____ Have   _____ Want   _____ Paid

87502 Mouse In A Treehole Candleholder/ Mouse Pulling A Mouse
RETIRED 1995
COMMENTS: Issued 1994, *Original Retail:* $17.00
Single candleholder; one of my very favorites.
Sec. Mkt.: $60 - 75

_____ Have   _____ Want   _____ Paid

87503 Mouse On Leaf Candleholder
RETIRED 1995
COMMENTS: Issued 1994, *Original Retail:* $17.00
The leaf is large; very beautiful piece.
Sec. Mkt.: $75 - 90

_____ Have   _____ Want   _____ Paid

87504 Mouse On Vine Candleholder
RETIRED 1995
COMMENTS: Issued 1994, *Original Retail:* $55.00
Very difficult to find, I suspect, because of cost and size. It measures 12" tall and is a tripod that holds three candles. Made of the same grapevine-like material as the baskets and ornament holder. Mouse in it is very large and tends to be poorly painted. Mouse can be found in different variations of brown. The price on this piece is subjective, as it's not being sold.
Sec. Mkt.: $300 - 325

_____ Have   _____ Want   _____ Paid

Deck the Halls/Squashville

87505 Mouse On Vine Wreath
RETIRED 1995

COMMENTS: Issued 1994, *Original Retail:* $55.00

The wreaths and the baskets are very hard to acquire. Usually found with light colored mouse.

Sec. Mkt.: $180 - 200

_____ Have   _____ Want   _____ Paid

87506 Mice On Vine Basket
RETIRED 1995

COMMENTS: Issued 1995, *Original Retail:* $55.00

You know what they say, "you can't have it all." Where would you keep it? Well, I am still searching for this one! There is a round and an oblong basket. Usually found with light colored mouse.

Sec. Mkt.: $185 - 200

_____ Have   _____ Want   _____ Paid

87509 Pyramid With Mice Candleholder/ Kerzenturm
RETIRED 1995

COMMENTS: Issued 1994, *Original Retail:* $40.00

This Kerzenturm (tower of lights) is made of balsa wood, and has two layers on the top. There are two mice kissing, and the bottom two mice are with an acorn. The windmill is supposed to spin when you light the six orange candles. Painting on these tends to be very poor. The mice are light in coloring on this piece.

Sec. Mkt.: $125 - 175

_____ Have   _____ Want   _____ Paid

Smiles and frowns cost nothing, but the difference in effect is enormous.

Deck the Halls/Squashville

87512 Snack For The Reindeer
RETIRED 1996

COMMENTS: Issued 1995, *Original Retail:* $13.00

How about Charming Tails Christmas cookies laid out on a Santa plate, a *Snack for the Reindeer*, and a glass of milk for your favorite Santa?

Sec. Mkt.: $18 - 20

_____ Have _____ Want _____ Paid

87529 Mouse On Basket
RETIRED 1995

COMMENTS: Issued 1994, *Original Retail:* $50.00

High retail, I suspect, is one of the reasons it is hard to find. Some retailers never ordered them. Light colored mouse appears on this figurine.

Sec. Mkt.: $175 - 200

_____ Have _____ Want _____ Paid

87532 Our First Christmas 1996
RETIRED 1996

COMMENTS: Issued 1996, *Original Retail:* $18.00

Look closely at the heads on these little mice to get them at the right angle on the sleigh. It looks like the body and the head had to be made in separate pieces.

Sec. Mkt.: $20 - 30

_____ Have _____ Want _____ Paid

87992 High Flying Mackenzie
RETIRED 1997

COMMENTS: Issued 1994, *Original Retail:* $21.00

This is the first piece we added to our collection. Some were mistakenly numbered as a limited edition. The original item number was 87002. 10,000 were produced numbered and numbered. In the future, look for it to reappear as a lapel pin bearing resemblance to *High Flying Mackenzie* and known as *Frequent Flyer*.

Sec. Mkt.: numbered - $35 - 50

not numbered - $25 - 30

_____ Have _____ Want _____ Paid

Nativity

87480   Li'l Drummer Mouse

COMMENTS: Issued 1996, *Original Retail:* $13.00

A lot of retailers and the catalog mistakenly included this reverent little mouse in the Parade. He belongs in the Nativity; look at his eyes. Check the drumsticks on this piece, they are very fragile.

Sec. Mkt.: $15

_____ Have   _____ Want   _____ Paid

87481   Angel Of Light

COMMENTS: Issued 1996, *Original Retail:* $13.00

The wings on the angel are copper like leaves, and are soldered together to make one piece. This piece is more difficult to find.

Sec. Mkt.: $15

_____ Have   _____ Want   _____ Paid

87482   Manger Animals

COMMENTS: Issued 1996, *Original Retail:* $21.00

The Squashville Gang improvised the other manger visitors with stuffed animals.

Sec. Mkt.: NE

_____ Have   _____ Want   _____ Paid

87546   Christmas Pageant Stage

COMMENTS: Issued 1996, *Original Retail:* $12.50

The little angel in the loft is exquisite. Wish they would make us some miniatures.

Sec. Mkt.: $40

_____ Have   _____ Want   _____ Paid

Nativity/Squashville

87547 Holy Family Players

COMMENTS: Issued 1995, *Original Retail:* $21.00

Maxine and Mackenzie play Mary and Joseph in their story of the first Christmas; a three piece set.

Sec. Mkt.: NE

_____ Have _____ Want _____ Paid

87548 Three Wise Mice

COMMENTS: Issued 1995, *Original Retail:* $21.00

Each mouse has brought the baby a present. Notice their wonderful crowns.

Sec. Mkt.: NE

_____ Have _____ Want _____ Paid

87710 Shepherd's Set

COMMENTS: Issued 1997, *Original Retail:* $12.50

These two are quite reverent in being added to the Nativity.

Sec. Mkt.: NE

_____ Have _____ Want _____ Paid

Choo Choo

87579   Charming Choo-Choo And Passenger

COMMENTS: Issued 1995, *Original Retail:* $36.00

There was some confusion in the original artwork, so the piece was produced as a single piece and had to be literally cut in half to allow the addition of the other cars. Otherwise, the caboose would have to be in the middle of the train! In the catalog, this piece has spokes on the train wheels.

Sec. Mkt.: $40

_____ Have _____ Want _____ Paid

87620   Reginald's Choo-Choo Ride

COMMENTS: Issued 1998, *Original Retail:* $19.00

Reginald is riding in a poinsettia. Lydia hitches a ride on his paw.

Sec. Mkt.: NE

_____ Have _____ Want _____ Paid

The Charming Choo Choo/Squashville

87694 Stewart's Choo-Choo Ride
COMMENTS: Issued 1996, *Original Retail:* $18.50

There is an error on this piece in the 1997 catalog. The leaf is attached with the bow in the back, but in the display page across from it, the bow is in the front.

Sec. Mkt.: $25

_____ Have   _____ Want   _____ Paid

87707 Chauncey's Choo-Choo
COMMENTS: Issued 1997, *Original Retail:* $19.00

Add Chauncey to the middle of the train; Binkey is the caboose.

Sec. Mkt.: NE

_____ Have   _____ Want   _____ Paid

Semi-Annual Midwest Collectibles Fest XV

Saturday, October 24, 1998
10 a.m. - 3 p.m.

Inland Meeting and Exposition Center
400 East Ogden Ave. • Westmont, IL 60559
(Accommodations – Club House Inn • 630-920-2200)
The largest show offering your favorite collectibles!
250 Tables plus!

Call!   For more Information call   *Call!*
1-800-445-8745 or 309-668-2211
Rosie Wells Enterprises, Inc.
22341 E. Wells Rd., Dept. MW • Canton, IL 61520

Squashville

87514 Testing The Lights
RETIRED 1997

COMMENTS: Issued 1996, *Original Retail:* $14.00
We all know how Reginald feels putting up the lights.
Sec. Mkt.: $18 - 25

_____ Have   _____ Want   _____ Paid

87521 Chestnut Chapel
RETIRED 1996

COMMENTS: Issued 1994, *Original Retail:* $45.00
All the houses are lit.
Sec. Mkt.: $51 - 60

_____ Have   _____ Want   _____ Paid

87522 Pumpkin Inn
SUSPENDED/RETIRED 1996

COMMENTS: Issued 1994, *Original Retail:* $48.00
Look this house over carefully. You will find it adorable! While it is usually found with an inscription, *Pumpkin Inn*, it can also be found spelled *Pumpkin Enn*.
Sec. Mkt.: $50 - 60

_____ Have   _____ Want   _____ Paid

87524 Old Cob Mill
LIMITED EDITION OF 75,000

COMMENTS: Issued 1994, *Original Retail:* $45.00
Sold out in 1996. This is the most sought after of the lighted houses.
Sec. Mkt.: $65 - 70

_____ Have   _____ Want   _____ Paid

Squashville

87533   Village Sign ☐

COMMENTS: Issued 1994, *Original Retail:* $31.00
Initially this piece didn't sell well, so many collectors were able to add it to their collection at half price.

Sec. Mkt.: $35 - 40

_____ Have   _____ Want   _____ Paid

87560   Mail Box, Bench ☐
SUSPENDED/RETIRED 1996

COMMENTS: Issued 1995, *Original Retail:* $12.00

These were included in some gift bags at the Florida Event.

Sec. Mkt.: $14 - 18

_____ Have   _____ Want   _____ Paid

87561   Street Light/Sign ☐
SUSPENDED

COMMENTS: Issued 1996, *Original Retail:* $12.00

Added to a gift bag given out by Fitz & Floyd, for the 1997 Florida Extravaganza, it can be found with the street name *Acorn Eve* instead of *Acorn Ave.*

Sec. Mkt.: NE

_____ Have   _____ Want   _____ Paid

Squashville

87562 Butternut Squash Dairy
LIMITED EDITION OF 7,500

COMMENTS: Issued 1995, *Original Retail:* $45.00

If you look around, you can still find some of the houses at retail.

Sec. Mkt.: $72 - 75

_____ Have _____ Want _____ Paid

87563 Mushroom Depot
SUSPENDED

COMMENTS: Issued 1996, *Original Retail:* $48.00

Notice the train tracks in front of the depot. Now you know where the *Charming Choo-Choo* is going!

Sec. Mkt.: $55 - 60

_____ Have _____ Want _____ Paid

87565 Pear Taxi
RETIRED 1996

COMMENTS: Issued 1995, *Original Retail:* $16.00

The *Pear Taxi* and the *Pear Candleholder* look cute together.

Sec. Mkt.: $24 - 30

_____ Have _____ Want _____ Paid

87569 Sleigh Ride
LIMITED EDITION OF 17,500

COMMENTS: Issued 1995, *Original Retail:* $16.00

Sold out in 1996; one of the more sought after pieces. It was released in limited edition in Canada, some without registration marks. Check the antlers on Mackenzie, they are very fragile. I have seen a lot of broken ones on the shelves.

Sec. Mkt.: $70 - 75

_____ Have _____ Want _____ Paid

Squashville

87572 Binkey's 1995 Ice Sculpture
RETIRED 1995

COMMENTS: Issued 1995, *Original Retail:* $20.00

A lot of these ended up half price, and now the collectors are beginning to wish they had run in to them! The price is slowly going up.

Sec. Mkt.: $30 - 32

_____ Have   _____ Want   _____ Paid

87573 Mail Mouse
RETIRED 1996

COMMENTS: Issued 1995, *Original Retail:* $12.00

Don't forget to put the *Mail Mouse* by the *Mailbox* in your display.

Sec. Mkt.: $24 - 30

_____ Have   _____ Want   _____ Paid

87583 Carrot Post Office
RETIRED 1996

COMMENTS: Issued 1995, *Original Retail:* $45.00

Put the *Mail Mouse* and the *Mailbox* with the *Post Office* and you have a darling scene; just add snow.

Sec. Mkt.: $45 - 48

_____ Have   _____ Want   _____ Paid

87584 Great Oak Town Hall
SUSPENDED/RETIRED 1996

COMMENTS: Issued 1995, *Original Retail:* $48.00

The houses, being more expensive, are slow to catch on. This is one of the only houses not limited.

Sec. Mkt.: $50 - 55

_____ Have   _____ Want   _____ Paid

Squashville

87590   Extra! Extra!
RETIRED 1997

COMMENTS: Issued 1996, *Original Retail:* $15.00

Add the *Newsstand* to this and have a wonderful scene!

Sec. Mkt.: $15 - 20

_____ Have   _____ Want   _____ Paid

87591   Reginald's Newsstand
RETIRED 1997

COMMENTS: Issued 1996, *Original Retail:* $21.00

Many didn't notice the charm of this piece until it became a little more work to add it to their collection. There are still a few out there if you look hard enough.

Sec. Mkt.: $25 - 30

_____ Have   _____ Want   _____ Paid

87597   Cantaloupe Cathedral
SUSPENDED

COMMENTS: Issued 1996, *Original Retail:* $48.00

Anybody catch the play on words? Can't elope.

Sec. Mkt.: $48 - 55

_____ Have   _____ Want   _____ Paid

87611   Candy Apple Candy Store
LIMITED EDITION OF 9,000

COMMENTS: Issued 1996, *Original Retail:* $48.00

Sold out. Houses are wonderful to add to your display!

Sec. Mkt.: $48 - 55

_____ Have   _____ Want   _____ Paid

Squashville

87621   Who Put That Tree There?

COMMENTS: Issued 1998, *Original Retail:* $16.50

Binkey is sledding into a pine tree.

Sec. Mkt.: NE

_____ Have   _____ Want   _____ Paid

87622   Merry Christmas From Our House To Yours

COMMENTS: Issued 1998, *Original Retail:* $23.00

Mackenzie in a little acorn house and *Binkey* in a carrot house are waving at each other.

Sec. Mkt.: NE

_____ Have   _____ Want   _____ Paid

87623   Team Igloo
LIMITED EDITION 1998

COMMENTS: Issued 1998, *Original Retail:* $23.00

Mackenzie is inside an igloo. Binkey is outside being handed ice by *Stewart* out the top of the igloo. With this piece, the painting of Stewart is becoming more refined and consistent. New pieces such as this one show him with less white. I think this looks really neat!

Sec. Mkt.: $25

_____ Have   _____ Want   _____ Paid

87624   Dashing Through The Snow

COMMENTS: Issued 1998, *Original Retail:* $16.50

Mackenzie is on a wooden sled coming through a snow drift. He left behind a mouse-shaped hole in the drift. I love it! A must have for collectors who first fell in love with Charming Tails after finding *Hot Doggin'* or *Maxine Making Snow Angels*.

Sec. Mkt.: NE

_____ Have   _____ Want   _____ Paid

Squashville

87625   Please, Just One More
COMMENTS: Issued 1998, *Original Retail:* $16.50

Mackenzie, who appears to be underdressed for the season, is putting ornaments on a leaning pine tree.

Sec. Mkt.: NE

_____ Have   _____ Want   _____ Paid

87690   Charming Tails Display Sign
COMMENTS: Issued 1997, *Original Retail:* $21.00

This piece has a stamped artist signature.

Sec. Mkt.: $25

_____ Have   _____ Want   _____ Paid

87704   Not A Creature Was Stirring
COMMENTS: Issued 1997, *Original Retail:* $17.50

The teddy bear is the same style as *You're Not Alone*.

Sec. Mkt.: $22

_____ Have   _____ Want   _____ Paid

87850   Baby's First 1996/
LIMITED EDITION
COMMENTS: Issued 1996, *Original Retail:* $13.00

Limited to year of production, not numbered. The little mouse in the pacifier is darling, dated 1996.

Sec. Mkt.: $18 - 22

_____ Have   _____ Want   _____ Paid

87925   Mackenzie and Maxine Caroling
RETIRED 1995
COMMENTS: Issued 1994, *Original Retail:* $18.00

The street lamp flashes. Small batteries are needed.

Found in earlier catalogs as *Maxine And Mickensy Caroling*.

Sec. Mkt.: $35 - 45

_____ Have   _____ Want   _____ Paid

Squashville

87947 Leaf Fence
SUSPENDED/RETIRED 1996

COMMENTS: Issued 1994, *Original Retail:* $7.00

Place beside your Squashville entrance sign. You may need to add more than one to your display!

Sec. Mkt.: $10 - 15

_____ Have   _____ Want   _____ Paid

87948 Acorn Street Lamp
SUSPENDED/RETIRED 1996

COMMENTS: Issued 1994, *Original Retail:* $6.00

You need a few of these to light up Squashville.

Sec. Mkt.: $7 - 10

_____ Have   _____ Want   _____ Paid

87993 Hot Doggin'
RETIRED 1995

COMMENTS: Issued 1994, *Original Retail:* $20.00

This signed piece was given to new members of the Acorn Society (a predecessor to the Leaf and Acorn Club), along with a tote bag, a cloisonné pin and a pen.

Sec. Mkt.: $32 - 35

_____ Have   _____ Want   _____ Paid

89700 Teacher's Pets

COMMENTS: Issued 1997, *Original Retail:* $19.50

Can you imagine a more perfect gift for a teacher's first day?

Sec. Mkt.: NE

_____ Have   _____ Want   _____ Paid

Squashville

89701   I'm Thinking Of You

COMMENTS: Issued 1997, *Original Retail:* $15.00

Lydia the ladybug makes an appearance again.

Sec. Mkt.: NE

_____ Have   _____ Want   _____ Paid

89702   Maxine Goes On Line

COMMENTS: Issued 1997, *Original Retail:* $17.00

Maxine is right in line with the times, talking Tails on line, I am sure! She has lots of friends on AOL.

Sec. Mkt.: NE

_____ Have   _____ Want   _____ Paid

89710   Keeping Our Love Alive

COMMENTS: Issued 1997, *Original Retail:* $19.50

There might be some errored pieces out there on this one. The terra cotta planter has holly on it and it isn't supposed to. Does yours?

Sec. Mkt.: NE

_____ Have   _____ Want   _____ Paid

89714   Guess What!

COMMENTS: Issued 1997, *Original Retail:* $16.50

Guess who is expecting; both pink and blue booties. A great baby gift!

Sec. Mkt.: NE

_____ Have   _____ Want   _____ Paid

89715   I Love You A Whole Bunch

COMMENTS: Issued 1997, Original Retail: $17.00

A little mouse has picked all the flower garden, but how could you scold her?

Sec. Mkt.: NE

_____ Have   _____ Want   _____ Paid

Trim A Tree

87203 Mackenzie Building Snowmouse
LIMITED EDITION OF 7,500

COMMENTS: Issued 1996, *Original Retail:* $18.00

Sold out in 1996. This piece has been found numbered and not numbered. It was issued in Canada without resgistration marks under the name Samaco. This piece is harder to find, so the missing registration mark has made little or no difference to the collector. Found in earlier catalogs as *Mickensy Building A Snow Mouse*.

Sec. Mkt.: $125 - 150

_____ Have   _____ Want   _____ Paid

87305 Flying Leaf Saucer
RETIRED *1996*

COMMENTS: Issued 1995, *Original Retail:* $17.00

This piece looks good with *Hot Doggin'*.

Sec. Mkt.: $25 - 35

_____ Have   _____ Want   _____ Paid

87426 Binkey In Bed Of Flowers
RETIRED *1996*

COMMENTS: Issued 1995, *Original Retail:* $15.00

Wouldn't he look cute with *Binkey's Poinsettia* in a centerpiece of poinsettias?

Sec. Mkt.: $25 - 35

_____ Have   _____ Want   _____ Paid

Trim a Tree/Squashville

87469   OOPS! Did I Do That? ☐
RETIRED 1997

COMMENTS: Issued 1996, *Original Retail:* $15.00

This is one of my favorites!! You can see Mackenzie's footprints in the cookie icing.

Sec. Mkt.: $20 - 30

_____ Have   _____ Want   _____ Paid

87471   All Wrapped Up ☐
LIMITED EDITION

COMMENTS: Issued 1996, *Original Retail:* $12.00

Limited to year of production. The tag on Mackenzie is dated.

Sec. Mkt.: $26 - 35

_____ Have   _____ Want   _____ Paid

87472   You Melted My Heart ☐
RETIRED 1996

COMMENTS: Issued 1995, *Original Retail:* $21.00

Left out of the 1996 catalog, so many collectors initially had a hard time finding it.

Sec. Mkt.: $25 - 30

_____ Have   _____ Want   _____ Paid

87483   Stamp Dispenser ☐

COMMENTS: Issued 1996, *Original Retail:* $12.00

Letter to Santa is a good companion for this piece. Look for this piece to retire soon!

Sec. Mkt.: $18

_____ Have   _____ Want   _____ Paid

At Christmas consider not so much the gift of a friend but the friendship of a giver.

Trim a Tree/Squashville

87496 Waiting For Christmas
LIMITED EDITION OF 14,000

COMMENTS: Issued 1996, *Original Retail:* $16.00

Sold out in 1996. This was a sleeper sell out; it just seemed to disappear.

Sec. Mkt.: $30 - 40

_____ Have   _____ Want   _____ Paid

87498 All I Can Give You Is Me
RETIRED 1996

COMMENTS: Issued 1996, *Original Retail:* $15.00

This one sold really well.

Sec. Mkt.: $35 - 45

_____ Have   _____ Want   _____ Paid

87500 My New Toy
RETIRED 1997

COMMENTS: Issued 1996, *Original Retail:* $15.00

Mackenzie seems to be enjoying his Christmas gift.

Sec. Mkt.: $15 - 20

_____ Have   _____ Want   _____ Paid

87501 Mouse Card Holder
RETIRED 1995

COMMENTS: Issued 1994, *Original Retail:* $13.00

This looks like a candle climber attached to a red velvet ribbon. I believe you are supposed to pin your cards to it.

Sec. Mkt.: $40 - 50

_____ Have   _____ Want   _____ Paid

Christmas holidays — anticipation, preparation, recreation, prostration and recuperation.

Trim a Tree/Squashville

87510 Maxine Making Snow Angels
RETIRED 1996

COMMENTS: Issued 1994, *Original Retail:* $21.00

Have you ever made snow angels? The feelings these little mice evoke are the reason collectors have become so passionate about them. *Maxine Making Snow Angels* seems to be responsible for starting a lot of collections. Maxine be found with a lighter color variation and the footprints may be found covered with snow.

Sec. Mkt.: $37 - 45

_____ Have _____ Want _____ Paid

87513 Jingle Bells
RETIRED 1997

COMMENTS: Issued 1996, *Original Retail:* $16.00

Stewart is tangled in sleigh bells.

Sec. Mkt.: $18 - 20

_____ Have _____ Want _____ Paid

87527 Peeking At Presents
RETIRED 1997

COMMENTS: Issued 1996, *Original Retail:* $14.00

Chauncey can't seem to contain his curiosity.

Sec. Mkt.: $18 - 20

_____ Have _____ Want _____ Paid

87566 Snow Plow
RETIRED 1996

COMMENTS: Issued 1995, *Original Retail:* $17.00

The attention to detail on Charming Tails makes them incredible. Look at the pile of snow in front of the plow.

Sec. Mkt.: $25 - 30

_____ Have _____ Want _____ Paid

Trim a Tree/Squashville

87570 The Snowball Fight
RETIRED 1996

COMMENTS: Issued 1995, *Original Retail:* $17.00

I don't know who is winning this snowball fight, but one of them needs a bigger tree to hide behind!

Sec. Mkt.: $25 - 28

_____ Have _____ Want _____ Paid

87571 Teamwork Helps!
RETIRED 1996

COMMENTS: Issued 1995, *Original Retail:* $17.00

There is more than one way to get the star on top of the tree.

Sec. Mkt.: $38 - 45

_____ Have _____ Want _____ Paid

87580 Binkey's Snow Shoeing
RETIRED 1996

COMMENTS: Issued 1995, *Original Retail:* $15.00

Look at the tracks in the snow that *Binkey* is leaving.

Sec. Mkt.: $24 - 30

_____ Have _____ Want _____ Paid

87598 Mouse Star Treetop
RETIRED 1995

COMMENTS: Issued 1993, *Original Retail:* $14.00

A must have for the top of your tree!

Sec. Mkt.: $53 - 60

_____ Have _____ Want _____ Paid

Trim a Tree/Squashville

87600 Bearing Gifts
COMMENTS: Issued 1996, *Original Retail:* $16.00

This was released in 1996 as a GCC early release, and released to other retailers in 1997.

Sec. Mkt.: $35 - 40

_____ Have _____ Want _____ Paid

87612 Maxine's Snowmobile Ride
COMMENTS: Issued 1996, *Original Retail:* $17.00

This was released in 1996 as a GCC early release and as part of the regular line in 1997. This is another difficult to find piece.

Sec. Mkt.: $20

_____ Have _____ Want _____ Paid

87692 Building a Snowbunny
COMMENTS: Issued 1996, *Original Retail:* $17.00

A great companion piece to *Building a Snowmouse*.

Sec. Mkt.: NE

_____ Have _____ Want _____ Paid

87695 Farmer Mackenzie
COMMENTS: Issued 1996, *Original Retail:* $17.00

Some what difficult to find, this is the cow's second appearance. He is also visiting the Nativity.

Sec. Mkt.: $20

_____ Have _____ Want _____ Paid

87698 Airmail
RETIRED 1997

COMMENTS: Issued 1996, *Original Retail:* $16.00

I think Stewart might help deliver the mail in places other than Squashville.

Sec. Mkt.: $18

_____ Have _____ Want _____ Paid

Trim a Tree/Squashville

87702 Trimming The Tree
COMMENTS: Issued 1997, *Original Retail:* $27.50
This is a wonderful value as a two piece set.
Sec. Mkt.: NE

_____ Have   _____ Want   _____ Paid

87703 All The Trimmings/ Trim A Tree Trail
RETIRED 1997
COMMENTS: Issued 1997, *Original Retail:* $15.00
Limited to year of production, not numbered. Retired at the end of 1997. *Trim A Tree Trail* was the name found in the catalog index.
Sec. Mkt.: $18 - 25

_____ Have   _____ Want   _____ Paid

87705 Baby's 1st Christmas 1997 Annual
RETIRED 1997
COMMENTS: Issued 1997, *Original Retail:* $18.50
This piece is an annual *Baby's 1st Christmas* piece. It was retired at year's end.
Sec. Mkt.: $20 - 22

_____ Have   _____ Want   _____ Paid

87714 Decorating Binkey
COMMENTS: Issued 1997, *Original Retail:* $16.00
This is hysterical!
Sec. Mkt.: NE

_____ Have   _____ Want   _____ Paid

If you have been going in circles, perhaps you have been cutting corners.

Trim a Tree/Squashville

87924 Binkey on Ice
RETIRED 1994

COMMENTS: Issued 1994, *Original Retail:* $10.00

Very hard to find, even on the secondary market. Both were issued under the same item number. Reginald seems to have more of a yellow coloring than later pieces.

Sec. Mkt.: $200 - 225

_____ Have   _____ Want   _____ Paid

87924 Reginald on Ice
RETIRED 1994

COMMENTS: Issued 1994, *Original Retail:* $10.00

Issued under the same item number as *Binkey on Ice*. Difficult to find.

Sec. Mkt.: $175 - 200

_____ Have   _____ Want   _____ Paid

87939 Holiday Wreath/Binkey
RETIRED 1995

COMMENTS: Issued 1993, *Original Retail:* $12.00

Issued under the same item number as mouse *Holiday Wreath/Mackenzie*. Some were found in cellophane packages with cardboard header. Found in earlier catalogs as *Bunny On Wreath*.

Sec. Mkt.: $37 - 45

_____ Have   _____ Want   _____ Paid

87939 Holiday Wreath/Mackenzie
RETIRED 1995

COMMENTS: Issued 1993, *Original Retail:* $12.00

Issued under the same item number as *Holiday Wreath/Binkey*. They hang by a small red string. Found in earlier catalogs as *Mouse On Wreath*.

Sec. Mkt.: $50 - 55

_____ Have   _____ Want   _____ Paid

Trim a Tree/Squashville

87940 Mackenzie Napping
RETIRED 1995

COMMENTS: Issued 1993, *Original Retail:* $12.00

One of the very early pieces. Found in earlier catalogs as *Mouse On Leaf Napping*.

Sec. Mkt.: $32 - 40

_____ Have _____ Want _____ Paid

87941 Hang In There
RETIRED 1996

COMMENTS: Issued 1993, *Original Retail:* $10.00

Mackenzie with tail down; mouse has a rubber tail. A great many have been found with the lighter color variation of mice. Found in earlier catalogs as *Mouse Hanger*.

Sec. Mkt.: $25 - 35

_____ Have _____ Want _____ Paid

87941 Hang In There
RETIRED 1996

COMMENTS: Issued 1993, *Original Retail:* $10.00

Mackenzie with berries; three with same item number. To date, there is no difference in value.

Sec. Mkt.: $25 - 35

_____ Have _____ Want _____ Paid

87941 Hang In There
RETIRED 1996

COMMENTS: Issued 1993, *Original Retail:* $10.00

Mackenzie with tail up; one of three issued with tail up. Also found with light and dark colored mice.

Sec. Mkt.: $25 - 35

_____ Have _____ Want _____ Paid

Trim a Tree/Squashville

87942 Maxine Lights A Candle
RETIRED 1995

COMMENTS: Issued 1993, *Original Retail:* $11.00

This ornament plugs into your light strand and lights up. Maxine is very tiny on the piece. Also issued under item number 87043. Found in earlier catalogs as *Mouse On Vine Lighted Ornament*.

Sec. Mkt.: $27 - 35

_____ Have _____ Want _____ Paid

87944 Mackenzie Snowball
LIMITED EDITION

COMMENTS: Issued 1994, *Original Retail:* $16.00

The 1994 on the snowball is done in red and charcoal. Neither is more valuable at this time, but red seems to be more difficult to find.

Sec. Mkt.: $60 - 75

_____ Have _____ Want _____ Paid

87969 Holiday Lights Ornament
RETIRED 1995

COMMENTS: Issued 1995, *Original Retail:* $10.00

There is also a yellow light bulb. Found in earlier catalogs as *Mouse On Red Light Bulb*.

Sec. Mkt.: $39 - 45

_____ Have _____ Want _____ Paid

87970 Mackenzie on Ice
RETIRED 1996

COMMENTS: Issued 1994, *Original Retail:* $10.00

The mouse in the old catalog is on the top of the icicle. Where is yours?

Sec. Mkt.: $45 - 50

_____ Have _____ Want _____ Paid

Trim a Tree/Squashville

87971   Friends In Flight
RETIRED 1994

COMMENTS: Issued 1994, *Original Retail:* $18.00

These are painted differently; they have cracks in the body. They are wonderful!

Sec. Mkt.: $93 - 100

_____ Have   _____ Want   _____ Paid

87991   Sticky Situations/
Mouse on Candy Cane
RETIRED 1996

COMMENTS: Issued 1994, *Original Retail:* $16.00

Two different pieces with the same item number.

Sec. Mkt.: $31 - 40

_____ Have   _____ Want   _____ Paid

87991   Sticky Situations/Ribbon Candy
RETIRED 1996

COMMENTS: Issued 1994, *Original Retail:* $16.00

Two with same item number. Neither is more valuable at this time.

Sec. Mkt.: $31 - 40

_____ Have   _____ Want   _____ Paid

Are Maxine and Mackenzie the only famous mice?

Here are some that we came up with:

Mickey and Minnie
Jerry from "Tom and Jerry"
Mighty Mouse
Speedy Gonzales
Pinkey and the Brain
A Computer Mouse
Feivel

Can you think of any more?

Waterglobes/Musicals

85778 Pumpkin Playtime
RETIRED 1995

COMMENTS: Issued 1995, *Original Retail:* $35.00

Plays: "*Whistle While You Work.*" The waterglobes took longer to catch on.

Sec. Mkt.: $70 - 90

_____ Have   _____ Want   _____ Paid

86790 Rocking Mice Musical
RETIRED 1994

COMMENTS: Issued 1993, *Original Retail:* $65.00

Plays: "*Have Yourself A Merry Little Christmas.*"
Very difficult to find. Also found in a pale version.

Sec. Mkt.: $185 - 200

_____ Have   _____ Want   _____ Paid

87200 Sailing Away
RETIRED 1994

COMMENTS: Issued 1993, *Original Retail:* $50.00

Plays: "*Anchors Away!*" The musicals have been slow to catch on. Although this musical was not limited, it has been reported that only 5,000 were produced.

Sec. Mkt.: $125 - 175

_____ Have   _____ Want   _____ Paid

87475 Baby's First Christmas Waterglobe
RETIRED 1996

COMMENTS: Issued 1996, *Original Retail:* $18.00

This piece was imited to one year of production. It was shown in the catalog in pastels, but produced in red and green. It is not known if any of the pastel ones were ever released, or if it was just a prototype.

Sec. Mkt.: $20 - 30

_____ Have   _____ Want   _____ Paid

Waterglobes & Musicals

87476   All Snug In Their Beds
RETIRED 1996
COMMENTS: Issued 1996, *Original Retail:* $30.00
Take a good look at the tiny bunnies inside the waterglobe. They are great!
Sec. Mkt.: $45 - 60

_____ Have   _____ Want   _____ Paid

87511   Skating Mouse Musical
RETIRED 1994
COMMENTS: Issued 1994, *Original Retail:* $25.00
Plays: "*Walking In A Winter Wonderland.*" This has the tiniest little mouse you can imagine! The mice are attached to a magnet that sits on the base spinning to the music.
Sec. Mkt.: $125 - 175

_____ Have   _____ Want   _____ Paid

87516   Trimming For The Tree Waterglobe
RETIRED 1994
COMMENTS: Issued 1994, *Original Retail:* $45.00
Collectors are picky about having a bubble in their waterglobe. If you are lucky enough to find this one at retail, take a chance on the bubble. It plays "Deck The Halls." There is some speculation that they were never fully filled. Very difficult to find. Found in earlier catalogs as *Trimmings For The Tree*.
Sec. Mkt.: $87 - 100

_____ Have   _____ Want   _____ Paid

87517   Sharing The Warmth
RETIRED 1994
COMMENTS: Issued 1994, *Original Retail:* $40.00
Plays: "*We Wish You A Merry Christmas.*"
Sec. Mkt.: $150 - 175

_____ Have   _____ Want   _____ Paid

Waterglobes & Musicals

87518 Letter To Santa/Waterglobe
RETIRED 1994

COMMENTS: Issued 1994, Original Retail: $45.00
Plays: "*Here Comes Santa Claus.*" If you look through the waterglobe you will see these adorable little fellows write the following, "Dear Santa, Pleeze Bring Cheeze." Found in the earlier catalogs as *Mice Writing Letter To Santa*.

Sec. Mkt.: $72 - 90

_____ Have   _____ Want   _____ Paid

87530 Together At Christmas
RETIRED 1995

COMMENTS: Issued 1994, Original Retail: $30.00

Hinged; says "Ivy Inn" on the outside and opens to reveal a tiny waterglobe with two small mice.

Sec. Mkt.: $87 - 95

_____ Have   _____ Want   _____ Paid

87534 Sweet Dreams Waterglobe
RETIRED 1994

COMMENTS: Issued 1994, Original Retail: $40.00

Plays : "*Have Yourself A Merry Little Christmas.*" He is asleep in a walnut shell, while the lullaby plays softly.

Sec. Mkt.: $100 - 125

_____ Have   _____ Want   _____ Paid

87542 Jawbreakers Musical
RETIRED 1995

COMMENTS: Issued 1994, Original Retail: $40.00

The gumball machine plays "*It's A Small World.*" Mackenzie is balancing a gumball on his nose.

Sec. Mkt.: $80 - 90

_____ Have   _____ Want   _____ Paid

Waterglobes & Musicals

87956 Mini Surprise Waterglobe
RETIRED 1994

COMMENTS: Issued 1994, *Original Retail:* $22.00

Heavy, hinged; opens up to a very small mouse. More appealing in person. Pictured above is waterglobe with lid on and with lid opened.

Sec. Mkt.: $66 - 75

_____ Have _____ Want _____ Paid

89555 Me Next!
RETIRED 1995

COMMENTS: Issued 1995, *Original Retail:* $45.00

Plays "*There Is No Place Like Home.*" One of the more difficult globes to find. It goes nicely with *Slumber Party* and *Feeding Time*.

Sec. Mkt.: $100 - 125

_____ Have _____ Want _____ Paid

89556 Underwater Explorer
RETIRED 1995

COMMENTS: Issued 1995, *Original Retail:* $45.00

The water in most is of a blueish tint. Plays "In The Good Old Summer Time."

Sec. Mkt.: $125 - 150

_____ Have _____ Want _____ Paid

Waterglobes & Musicals

89557   My Hero!
RETIRED 1995

COMMENTS: Issued 1994, *Original Retail:* $45.00

One little mouse is saving an overboard mouse. Plays "*It's A Small World.*"

Sec. Mkt.: $100 - 125

_____ Have   _____ Want   _____ Paid

89602   Up, Up And Away
RETIRED 1995

COMMENTS: Issued 1994, *Original Retail:* $70.00

Of a higher retail price, but a magnificent piece. The butterfly rocks back and forth to the tune "*Up, Up and Away,*" of course!

Sec. Mkt.: $160 - 180

_____ Have   _____ Want   _____ Paid

92224   Mouse On Cheese
RETIRED 1995

COMMENTS: Issued 1994, *Original Retail:* $44.00

Very difficult to find.

Sec. Mkt.: $300 - 350

_____ Have   _____ Want   _____ Paid

92225   Mouse on Rubber Duck Waterglobe
RETIRED 1995

COMMENTS: Issued 1994, *Original Retail:* $44.00

Plays "*Rubber Ducky*" of course.

Sec. Mkt.: $90 - 125

_____ Have   _____ Want   _____ Paid

Collectibles Database™

The Best Collecting Software for Collectors
Stay organized with Collectibles Database!
FEATURING PRICE GUIDES FROM ROSIE WELLS ENTERPRISES, INC.,
Collectors' Society of America, J. Phillip, Inc., and other respected Price Guide Publishers.

Create insurance reports, inventory lists, want lists. Unlimited reporting capabilities.

Include your own images and long comments. Unlimited searching and sorting capabilities.

30 day money back guarantee. IBM compatible, 486 or better, 4 MB RAM or better (Mac with SoftWindows).

Telephone technical support, printed manual and on-screen help.

Easier to install and use! Super help! Just call from your home!

The values in this guide are in this software program!

$49.95

$49.95 + $5 Shipping & Handling
(includes 1 software price guide - your choice)
Additional software guides $15 each.

PRICE GUIDES AVAILABLE FOR:

Charming Tails™, Beanie Babies™ (includes color photos), Boyds Collection, Hallmark Ornaments (includes color photos), Hallmark Kiddie Car Classics™ (includes color photos), Hallmark Merry Miniatures® (includes color photos), Radko Ornaments, Precious Moments® Collectibles (includes color, licensed photos), Swarovski, Cherished Teddies® (includes color, licensed photos), Walt Disney Classics, Forma Vitrum (includes color photos), Memories Of Yesterday®, Shelia's Collectibles, Harbour Lights, Precious Moments™ Applause® Dolls and Longaberger® Baskets (includes color photos)! Hallmark Tender Touches List available.

For Technical Support, phone 703/777-5660
E-mail at Belofsky@MSDATABASE.com

Rosie Wells Enterprises, Inc.

22341 E. Wells Rd. • Canton, IL 61520 • http://www.RosieWells.com
Phone: 800/445-8745 • Fax: 309/668-2795

Club Offerings

Acorn Society Pin/Tote/Pen/Hot Doggin' Signed
RETIRED 1997

COMMENTS: Issued 1996, Retail: *$10.00*

This is a cloisonné pin with nice detail. It was given as part of the Acorn Society that was started exclusively at the Rosemont, Illinois, and Long Beach, California, shows. This was the predecessor to the Leaf and Acorn Club; a tote, a felt pen and an autographed *Hot Doggin'*. This piece is a Society Gift.

Sec. Mkt.: $50 - 80

_____ Have   _____ Want   _____ Paid

98700   Thank You
RETIRED 1998

COMMENTS: Issued 1997, *Original Retail:* $24.50

Included with the charter membership in The Leaf and Acorn Club. Also included was *Caps Off To You* resin pin. Charter year was extended to 1997-1998.

Sec. Mkt.: $30

_____ Have   _____ Want   _____ Paid

Coming together is a beginning; keeping together is progress; working together is success.

Club

98701 Maxine's Leaf Collection
1997 Charter Members Only

COMMENTS: Issued 1998, *Original Retail:* $15.00

Only available with Charter membership in The Leaf and Acorn Club, then available to purchase with a redemption form. Maxine is looking at a gold leaf.

Sec. Mkt.: $25

_____ Have _____ Want _____Paid

97/12 A Growing Friendship

COMMENTS: Issued 1998, *Original Retail:* $17.00

Members only redemption piece.

Sec. Mkt.: $25

_____ Have _____ Want _____Paid

Added Attractions

87601   Sending A Little Snow Your Way
FALL GCC EXCLUSIVE
COMMENTS: Issued 1996, *Original Retail:* $15.00
Fall GCC special one day event figurine.
Sec. Mkt.: $20 - 30

_____ Have _____ Want _____ Paid

87691   Take Me Home
RETIRED 1996
COMMENTS: Issued 1996, *Original Retail:* $17.00
It is reported only 4,800 were produced.
Sec. Mkt.: $44 - 50

_____ Have _____ Want _____ Paid

87862   Love Blooms
SPRING GCC EXCLUSIVE
COMMENTS: Issued 1996, *Original Retail:* $16.50
GCC is Gift Creations Concepts. They have offered a one day special event piece in the spring and in the fall. This was the first GCC piece.
Sec. Mkt.: $31.50 - 40

_____ Have _____ Want _____ Paid

Added Attractions

89562 Maxine Picking Strawberries
NALED EXCLUSIVE
COMMENTS: Issued 1994, *Original Retail:* $12.00
Also issued under *Mouse In The Strawberry*.
Sec. Mkt.: $45 - 50

_____ Have   _____ Want   _____ Paid

98195 One Mouse Open Sleigh
FALL GCC EXCLUSIVE
COMMENTS: Issued 1997, *Original Retail:* $17.50
Only available November 15, 1997. However, some GCC dealers may have overstocked them, so it may be found at retail with some searching.
Sec. Mkt.: $20 - 25

_____ Have   _____ Want   _____ Paid

98196 Mackenzie The Snowman
PARKWEST, NALED EXCLUSIVE
COMMENTS: Issued 1997, *Original Retail:* $17.00
This piece was limited to select catalog retailers.
Sec. Mkt.: $25 - 45

_____ Have   _____ Want   _____ Paid

98197 I Picked This Just For You
LIMITED EDITION OF 4,800
COMMENTS: Issued 1997, *Original Retail:* $18.00
Available for purchase at Charming Tails signing events, Dean Griff signed them.
Sec. Mkt.: $45 - 50

_____ Have   _____ Want   _____ Paid

Added Attractions

98198 Life Is A Bed Of Roses

COMMENTS: Issued 1998, *Original Retail:* $19.00

Signing Piece for 1998. Reportedly, only 4,800-5,000 pieces produced. A very exquisite piece, sure to be a favorite for many.

Sec. Mkt.: $25

_____ Have   _____ Want   _____ Paid

98200 Peek-A-Boo In The Posies
SPRING GCC EXCLUSIVE

COMMENTS: Issued 1998, *Original Retail:* $20.00

GCC Spring Exclusive; limited to May 2, 1998.

Sec. Mkt.: $30

_____ Have   _____ Want   _____ Paid

98202 Mackenzie's Holiday Hat
1998 PARKWEST EXCLUSIVE

COMMENTS: Issued 1998, *Original Retail:* $18.

Exclusive to Parkwest dealers. Picture was not available at press time. Mackenzie is sitting inside a Santa hat.

Sec. Mkt.: NE

_____ Have   _____ Want   _____ Paid

Picture not available

98204 My Spring Bonnet...
1998 SPRING CATALOG EXCLUSIVE

COMMENTS: Issued 1998, *Original Retail:* $18.50

1998 Spring Catalog Exclusive.

Sec. Mkt.: $25

_____ Have   _____ Want   _____ Paid

Added Attractions

98208 A Collection Of Friends
MCRAND SHOW EXCLUSIVE OF 7,500

COMMENTS: Issued 1998, *Original Retail:* $22.00

This piece was issued in the spring of 1998 for the International Gift Show. It was also available at Rosemont, IL. If you missed this piece at the show, you will only find it on the secondary market after these shows. This is an honor to be chosen from all the artists represented at these shows. Mackenzie, Reginald, Snail, Butterfly on a rug and Lady Bug on a rug, reading a book. This piece is said to be hand-numbered.

Sec. Mkt.: $50 - 70

_____ Have _____ Want _____ Paid

98600 Hang On
SPRING GCC EXCLUSIVE

COMMENTS: Issued 1997, *Original Retail:* $20.00.

There is substantial variation in the painting on these, so if you have a choice, look them over.

Sec. Mkt.: $25 - 30

_____ Have _____ Want _____ Paid

98929 You Are Not Alone
RETIRED 1996

COMMENTS: Issued 1995, *Original Retail:* $20.00

A portion of the proceeds on this piece go to Aids Service Organizations. Look for future charity pieces from a benevolent artist!

Sec. Mkt.: $45 - 65

_____ Have _____ Want _____ Paid

Subscribe to the Collector's Bulletin™

Accessories

89610   Pink Columbine

89611   Yellow Lily

COMMENTS: Issued 1996, *Original Retail:* $22.50

These ornament hangers were used in the 1996 catalog to display the Charming Tails line. They are lovely display pieces. Not designed by Dean Griff.

Sec. Mkt.: $25

_____ Have   _____ Want   _____ Paid

87519   Leaf Vine Ornament Hanger
        RETIRED 1995

COMMENTS: Issued 1994, *Original Retail:* $25.00

This is made of grapevine-like material, cloth and wire leaves and some red berries. Looks good holding one of the leaf ornaments.

Sec. Mkt.: $45

_____ Have   _____ Want   _____ Paid

Accessories

81/1 - 81/4 Fall and the Squashville Christmas Parade, Harvest, Winter Holiday, Variety, Spring and EveryDay

COMMENTS: Issued 1997, *Original Retail:* $30.00 ea.

The general consensus on these was they were too dark. They were not drawn by Dean, but used for display.

Sec. Mkt.: NE

_____ Have   _____ Want   _____ Paid

San Francisco Music Box Co.

41450182   Waterslide ☐
COMMENTS: Issued 1996, *Original Retail:* $39.95
Plays: "*A Whole New World.*"
Sec. Mkt.: $45

_____ Have   _____ Want   _____ Paid

4145095   Reach For The Stars ☐
DISCONTINUED
COMMENTS: Issued 1995, *Original Retail:* $35.00
Plays: "*When You Wish Upon A Star.*"
Sec. Mkt.: $60

_____ Have   _____ Want   _____ Paid

41451108   Catchin' Butterflies ☐
COMMENTS: Issued 1996, *Original Retail:* $34.95
Plays: "*Edelweiss.*"
Sec. Mkt.: $40

_____ Have   _____ Want   _____ Paid

41451223   Midday Snooze ☐
COMMENTS: Issued 1996, *Original Retail:* $34.95
Plays: "*I Dream A Dream*" from "Les Miserables." My tag on the bottom of this one says, "handcrafted for Charming Tails Made in China."
Sec. Mkt.: $40

_____ Have   _____ Want   _____ Paid

San Francisco Music Box

41451231 Hangin' Around ☐
COMMENTS: Issued 1997, *Original Retail:* $34.95
Plays: "*It's A Small World After All.*"
Sec. Mkt.: $60

_____ Have _____ Want _____ Paid

41454090 I'm Berry Happy ☐
COMMENTS: Issued 1996, *Original Retail:* $34.95
Plays: "*My Favorite Things.*"
Sec. Mkt.: $45

_____ Have _____ Want _____ Paid

41454125 Bunny Buddies ☐
COMMENTS: Issued 1997, *Original Retail:* $35.00
Plays: "*Getting To Know You.*"
Sec. Mkt.: $45

_____ Have _____ Want _____ Paid

41470249 Everyone Needs A Hand/ ☐
Thanks For Being There
COMMENTS: Issued 1995, *Original Retail:* $35.00
Plays: "*That's What Friends Are For.*" Sold out.
Sec. Mkt.: $55

_____ Have _____ Want _____ Paid

4147023100 Springtime Flowers/ ☐
Yellow
DISCONTINUED
COMMENTS: Issued 1995, *Original Retail:* $35.00
Plays: "*You Are My Sunshine.*"
Sec. Mkt.: $55

_____ Have _____ Want _____ Paid

Giftware by Silvestri

Halloween
DISCONTINUED

COMMENTS: Issued 1996, *Original Retail:* $7 - $25 ea.

Note, not all figurines are pictured above. Unsure of distribution on these also:

86868	**Trick Or Treat Witch Ghost**	☐
86871	**Ghost In Pumpkin Candleholder**	☐
86876	**Ghost Eating Treats**	☐
86879	**Reading Ghost Stories**	☐
86881	**Witch Asleep With Kitten**	☐
86884	**Witch Carrying Kitten**	☐
86994	**A Ride To The Moon Musical**	☐
	Plays: *Music Of The Night from Phantom of the Opera.*	
86995	**Kitten w/Pumpkin Candleholder Facing Away From Candle**	☐
86995	**Kitten w/Pumpkin Candleholder Facing Candle**	☐
86996	**Kitten In Pumpkin**	☐
86998	**Kitten w/Witch Hat**	☐

Sec. Mkt.: $15 - $60

_____ Have _____ Want _____ Paid

Giftware by Silvestri

Peppermint Bears
DISCONTINUED

COMMENTS: Issued 1996, *Original Retail:* $12 - $22 ea.

These pieces released were very limited, due to Fitz & Floyd acquiring the *Charming Tails*™ line. Only a sampling of figurines are pictured above. Following are the ones I am aware of:

47000	**Bear In Teacup Figurine**	☐
47018	**Bear w/Peppermint Skis Ornament**	☐
47019	**Bear On Teapot Train**	☐
47027	**Bear On Peppermint Horse**	☐
47030	**Bear In Teacup Sled Ornament**	☐
47031	**Bear Angel Ornament**	☐
47041	**Bear In Saucer Ornament**	☐
47043	**Gift Box Bear Ornaments (2 items, same number)**	☐
	Yo Yo, White Bell w/Peppermint	☐ ☐
470202	**Baby's First Bear in Teacup Ornament**	☐

Sec. Mkt.: $20 - $50

_____ Have _____ Want _____ Paid

Giftware by Silvestri

Snow Makers
DISCONTINUED

COMMENTS: Issued 1996, *Original Retail:* $15 - $45 ea.

5211	Elf Jumping Snowflake Rope	☐	52126	Small Elf Ornament
52092	Cardinal On Candy Cane	☐		(3 styles) ☐ ☐ ☐
52094	Elf w/Snowflake Beard	☐	52130	Elf w/Bag Of Snowflakes ☐
52108	Elf Rolling/Cutting Snowflakes		52135	Cardinal Nest
	(2 styles) ☐ ☐			(2 styles) ☐ ☐
52109	Elf On Snowflake Sled	☐	52139	Cardinal Nest/Eggs ☐
52110	Elf In Snowflake	☐	52140	Elf On Bell ☐
52112	Elf Tree w/Snow Star	☐	52142	Mini Elf Snowflake
52114	Elf Stocking/Mitten			(2 styles) ☐ ☐
	(2 styles) ☐ ☐		52550	Elf Ornament Holder ☐
52118	Elf And Cardinal On Branch	☐	52551	Elves Warming Up Around Votive ☐
52119	Elf Sliding Down Icicle	☐	52552	Elf Pulling Leaf w/Cardinal ☐
52120	Elf/Cardinal In Snow nest		52570	Elf Candleholders, Pair ☐
	(2 Styles) ☐ ☐		52571	Snow Elf Mini Waterglobe ☐
52121	Tiny Elf In Bell	☐	52572	Elf In Tree Candleholder ☐
52123	Tiny Elf In Snowflake	☐	66213	Cardinal Icicle ☐
52124	Elf Painting Snowflakes Ornament	☐		
52125	Elves/Snowflakes			
	(2 styles) ☐ ☐			

Sec. Mkt.: $25 - $70

_____ Have   _____ Want   _____ Paid

Giftware by Silvestri

51605   Stag Candleholder
DISCONTINUED
COMMENTS: Issued 1996, *Original Retail:* $25.00

It is questionable that these were ever distributed in the regular line.

Sec. Mkt.: $75 - 100

_____ Have   _____ Want   _____ Paid

86867   Three Leaf Candleholder
DISCONTINUED
COMMENTS: Issued 1997, *Original Retail:* $12.00

Given to guests at the Florida Extravaganza, in 1997, as part of their gift bags.

Sec. Mkt.: $25 - 50

_____ Have   _____ Want   _____ Paid

86874   Acorn Leaf Candleholder
DISCONTINUED
COMMENTS: Issued 1996, *Original Retail:* $12.00

This has an acorn nested; holds a candle in the brown leaf.

Sec. Mkt.: $55 - 60

_____ Have   _____ Want   _____ Paid

86885   Squash Gourd Candleholder
DISCONTINUED
COMMENTS: Issued 1996, *Original Retail:* $12.00

It is questionable if these pieces were ever released in full distribution. Has the yellow and green squash, and an orange pumpkin holds the candle.

Sec. Mkt.: $55 - 60

_____ Have   _____ Want   _____ Paid

Giftware by Silvestri

88543   Small Bunny Candleholder
DISCONTINUED

COMMENTS: Issued 1996, *Original Retail:* $10.00

This is a very small piece. It holds a single taper and is a single style candleholder.

Sec. Mkt.: $25 - 35

_____ Have   _____ Want   _____ Paid

88545   Basket Of Bunnies
DISCONTINUED

COMMENTS: Issued 1995, *Original Retail:* $18.95

There was also a Roman basket of bunnies with brown bunnies.

Sec. Mkt.: $35 - 45

_____ Have   _____ Want   _____ Paid

88546   Bunny Egg Topper
DISCONTINUED

COMMENTS: Issued 1996, *Original Retail:* $9.95

Two separate pieces; the bottom legs are a place to set an egg and the head is placed on top.

Sec. Mkt.: $25 - 30

_____ Have   _____ Want   _____ Paid

88555   Yellow Duck Egg Topper
DISCONTINUED

COMMENTS: Issued 1996, *Original Retail:* $9.95

The egg in the middle makes the body of the animal.

Sec. Mkt.: $25 - 30

_____ Have   _____ Want   _____ Paid

Giftware by Silvestri

88560 Little Lamb Egg Topper
DISCONTINUED
COMMENTS: Issued 1996, *Original Retail:* $9.95

This is the only lamb that I have seen. Maybe there will be more later. He is really cute!

Sec. Mkt.: $25 - 30

_____ Have   _____ Want   _____ Paid

88787 Easter Egg Candleholder
DISCONTINUED
COMMENTS: Issued 1996, *Original Retail:* $18.00

There is a stack of four Easter eggs, three of which hold candles. It is one of the largest pieces.

Sec. Mkt.: $45 - 65

_____ Have   _____ Want   _____ Paid

88791 Bunny Bunch of Flowers
DISCONTINUED
COMMENTS: Issued 1996, *Original Retail:* $15.00

Confused a lot in the beginning with the *Bunny Daffodil Candleholder*. It helped once there were pictures to put with them.

Sec. Mkt.: $40 - 55

_____ Have   _____ Want   _____ Paid

What every mouse wants... cheese!

Giftware by Silvestri

88794   Bunny Trio
DISCONTINUED

COMMENTS: Issued 1996, *Original Retail:* $15.00

Single style candleholder. The tips of the grass blades are delicate.

Sec. Mkt.: $45 - 60

_____ Have   _____ Want   _____ Paid

89408   Bunny Basket Trinket Box
DISCONTINUED

COMMENTS: Issued 1996, *Original Retail:* $15.00

This is a trinket box, just the right size to stash your rings in.

Sec. Mkt.: $35 - 45

_____ Have   _____ Want   _____ Paid

89409   Easter Egg Trinket Box
DISCONTINUED

COMMENTS: Issued 1996, *Original Retail:* $15.00

This is a delightful box! Take the gray bunny off and there is a small compartment to stash a tiny treasure.

Sec. Mkt.: $35 - 45

_____ Have   _____ Want   _____ Paid

89411   Bunny Butterfly
Candleholders/Awake
DISCONTINUED

COMMENTS: Issued 1996, *Original Retail:* $12.50

This is a strange thing. I have found some in boxes, paired and labeled a set, and some in individual boxes. Watch how you find them.

Sec. Mkt.: $35 - 40

_____ Have   _____ Want   _____ Paid

Giftware by Silvestri

89411 Bunny Butterfly
Candleholders/Asleep
DISCONTINUED

COMMENTS: Issued 1996, *Original Retail:* $12.50

The bunny on this one is sitting down, asleep with a butterfly on his ears.

Sec. Mkt.: $35 - 40

_____ Have _____ Want _____ Paid

89412 Small Carrot Candleholder
Candleholders/Asleep
DISCONTINUED

COMMENTS: Issued 1996, *Original Retail:* $13.00

There is also a carrot candleholder in the regular *Charming Tails*™ line, however, this is much smaller, around 2" in height.

Sec. Mkt.: $40 - 50

_____ Have _____ Want _____ Paid

88792 Bunny Daffodil Egg
DISCONTINUED

COMMENTS: Issued 1996, *Original Retail:* $10.00

Two different eggs with the same item number.

Sec. Mkt.: $30 - 40

_____ Have _____ Want _____ Paid

88792 Bunny Iris Egg
DISCONTINUED

COMMENTS: Issued 1995, *Original Retail:* $10.00

The bunny is sitting on four legs on this one. On the other egg, the bunny is standing.

Sec. Mkt.: $30 - 40

_____ Have _____ Want _____ Paid

Giftware by Roman

Bunnies In Diapers
DISCONTINUED
COMMENTS: Issued 1997, *Original Retail:* $6 - $12 ea.

Unsure of distribution on these also:

63605	Boy Bunny On Flower/Girl Bunny On Flower	☐
63606	Two Bunnies/Eggcup	☐
63610	Playing Bunnies/Egg Holder	☐
63613	Bunny Doctor	☐
63614	Bunny Fireman	☐
63615	Bunny Cowboy	☐
63616	Bunny Police	☐
63649	Bunny In Teacup	☐
63095	Basket W/Diapers	☐

Sec. Mkt.: $20 - $55

_____ Have _____ Want _____ Paid

Giftware by Roman

64238 Four Chipmunks Yawning Waterglobe
DISCONTINUED

COMMENTS: Issued 1994, *Original Retail:* $45.00
Plays "Brahms Lullaby" and has a tree trunk base.
Sec. Mkt.: $200 - 225

_____ Have _____ Want _____ Paid

67337 Bear On Glass Ball Ornament
DISCONTINUED

COMMENTS: Issued 1994, *Original Retail:* $10.00
The bear on this is much different than the other bear ornaments.
Sec. Mkt.: $55 - 65

_____ Have _____ Want _____ Paid

Blowing Bubbles
DISCONTINUED

COMMENTS: Issued 1994,
Original Retail: $6.50 - $10 ea.

67338	**Chipmunk Blowing Bubbles**
69488	**Skunk With Bubbles**
69489	**Squirrel Bubbles**

Sec. Mkt.: $20 - 25

_____ Have _____ Want _____ Paid

69186 Bird On Ice Cube Ornament
DISCONTINUED

COMMENTS: Issued 1995, *Original Retail:* $8.00
Three different styles, same item number.
Sec. Mkt.: $18 - 30

_____ Have _____ Want _____ Paid

69195 Candy Cane Birdhouse Ornament
DISCONTINUED

COMMENTS: Issued 1995, *Original Retail:* $8.00
Two styles with same item numbers.
Sec. Mkt.: $12 - 15

_____ Have _____ Want _____ Paid

Giftware by Roman

69207 Woodpecker On Cookie Ornament
DISCONTINUED

COMMENTS: Issued 1995, *Original Retail:* $7.00

This puts you in mind of Christmas cookies. The woodpecker is darling!

Sec. Mkt.: $20 - 30

_____ Have   _____ Want   _____ Paid

69243 Marble Ornaments
DISCONTINUED

COMMENTS: Issued 1995, *Original Retail:* $4.50

About 1" in size; *Frog*, *Chipmunk*, *Opossum*, *Bear*, *Fox* and *Squirrel*.

Sec. Mkt.: $10 - 15

_____ Have   _____ Want   _____ Paid

69244 Santa Tangled In Lights Ornament
DISCONTINUED

COMMENTS: Issued 1995, *Original Retail:* $8.00

Will also stand. Cataloged as part of the *Clumsy Claus* series.

Sec. Mkt.: $15 - 20

_____ Have   _____ Want   _____ Paid

Giftware by Roman

69264 Thimble Ornaments
DISCONTINUED
COMMENTS: Issued 1995, *Original Retail:* $3.00
Miniatures, about 1"; *Fox, Chipmunk, Frog* and *Bear*.
Sec. Mkt.: $8 - 12

_____ Have _____ Want _____ Paid

67319 Diet?... Tomorrow
DISCONTINUED
COMMENTS: Issued 1995, *Original Retail:* $7.50
Cataloged as part of the *Clumsy Claus* series.
Sec. Mkt.: $15 - 20

_____ Have _____ Want _____ Paid

69421 Bear On Snowflake/ Fox On Snowflake/ Chipmunk On Snowflake
DISCONTINUED
COMMENTS: Issued 1995, *Original Retail:* $3.50
Similar to *Mackenzie* on the snowflake.
Sec. Mkt.: $8 - 15

_____ Have _____ Want _____

To find older Charming Tails, Silvestri or Roman figurines, advertise in the Weekly Collectors' Gazette™.

Giftware by Roman

**69422 Bear on Candy Cane/
Chipmunk on Candy Cane/
Fox on Candy Cane**
DISCONTINUED
COMMENTS: Issued 1995, *Original Retail:* $4.00
Sec. Mkt.: $8 - 15

_____ Have   _____ Want   _____ Paid

**69423 Bear On Holly Leaf/
Chipmunk On Holly Leaf/
Fox On Holly Leaf**
DISCONTINUED
COMMENTS: Issued 1995, *Original Retail:* $3.50
These are darling miniature ornaments!
Sec. Mkt.: $10 - 15

_____ Have   _____ Want   _____ Paid

69612 Cat With Button
DISCONTINUED
COMMENTS: Issued 1995, *Original Retail:* $3.00
Measures $2^1/_2$".
Sec. Mkt.: $10 - 15

_____ Have   _____ Want   _____ Paid

Giftware by Roman

69613   Dog In Thimble
DISCONTINUED

COMMENTS: Issued 1995, *Original Retail:* $3.00

Very heavy; the dog is sitting in the thimble.

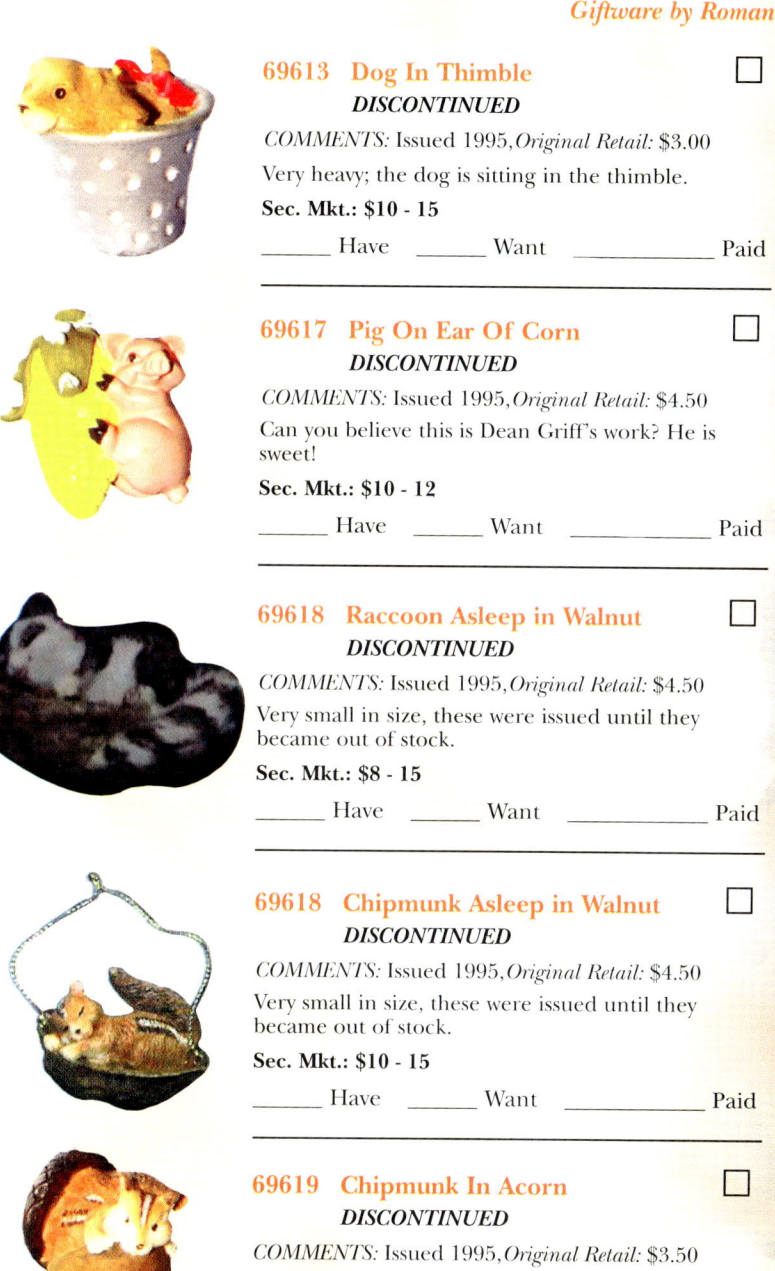

Sec. Mkt.: $10 - 15

_____ Have   _____ Want   _____ Paid

69617   Pig On Ear Of Corn
DISCONTINUED

COMMENTS: Issued 1995, *Original Retail:* $4.50

Can you believe this is Dean Griff's work? He is sweet!

Sec. Mkt.: $10 - 12

_____ Have   _____ Want   _____ Paid

69618   Raccoon Asleep in Walnut
DISCONTINUED

COMMENTS: Issued 1995, *Original Retail:* $4.50

Very small in size, these were issued until they became out of stock.

Sec. Mkt.: $8 - 15

_____ Have   _____ Want   _____ Paid

69618   Chipmunk Asleep in Walnut
DISCONTINUED

COMMENTS: Issued 1995, *Original Retail:* $4.50

Very small in size, these were issued until they became out of stock.

Sec. Mkt.: $10 - 15

_____ Have   _____ Want   _____ Paid

69619   Chipmunk In Acorn
DISCONTINUED

COMMENTS: Issued 1995, *Original Retail:* $3.50

The Chipmunk is peeping out; hangs by a gold cord.

Sec. Mkt.: $12 - 15

_____ Have   _____ Want   _____ Paid

Giftware by Roman

69619   Raccoon In Acorn ☐
DISCONTINUED
COMMENTS: Issued 1995, *Original Retail:* $4.50
Pieces are very heavy.
Sec. Mkt.: $10 - 15
_____ Have   _____ Want   _____ Paid

Chipmunk Stocking Holder ☐
DISCONTINUED
COMMENTS: Issued 1994, *Original Retail:* $24.50
Very heavy; sits on a ledge to hold your stocking.
Sec. Mkt.: $275 - 300
_____ Have   _____ Want   _____ Paid

On Wings Of Love

One calm, sunshiny day an Angel ventured out of heaven to find the most enduring of all things on earth. He roamed field and forest, city and hamlet, and just as the sun went down, he plumed his wings and said: "Now my visit is over, and I must go back to the heaven of light. But before I go I must gather some mementos of my visit on earth."

He looked over into a beautiful flower garden, and said, "How lovely and fragrant these flowers are." He plucked the rarest roses, and made a bouquet and said, "I see nothing more beautiful than these: I will take them with me."

But he looked a little farther, and saw a little bright-eyed rosy-cheeked baby smiling into its mother's face, and he said, "Oh that baby's smile is prettier than this bouquet: I will take that, too."

Then he looked just beyond the cradle and there was a mother's love pouring out toward the baby like the gush of a river, and he said, " Oh that mother's love is the most enduring thing I have seen on earth." I will carry that back with me, too."

With the three treasures he winged his way to the pearly gates, and said, "Before I go in, I will examine my mementos." He looked at the flowers, and they had withered; he looked at the baby's smile, and it had faded to tears: he looked at the mother's love, and there it was in all its pristine beauty and fragrance! The Angel threw aside the withered flowers, and the faded smile, then winged his way through the gates, called all the hosts of heaven together, and said:

"Here is the only thing I found on earth that would keep its beauty all the way to heaven, "a mothers love."

Giftware by Roman

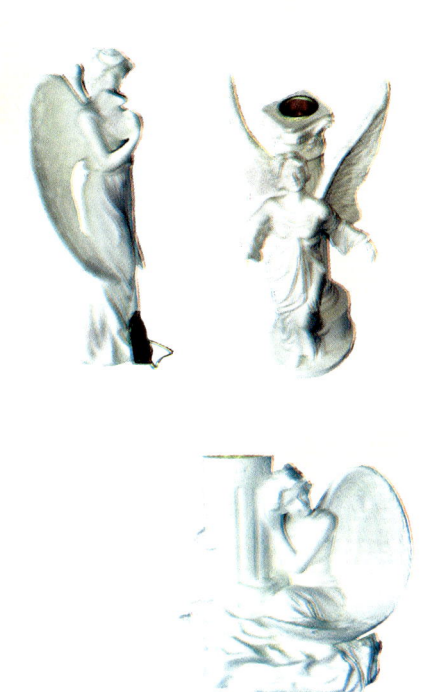

White Angels

DISCONTINUED

COMMENTS: Isssued 1995, *Original Retail:* $10 - $50

The above is a sampling of the white alabaster type angels that Dean Griff did for Roman. They are very elegant and put you in mind of Greek art. Some of them were still available as late as 1996. The item numbers of most were changed as time progressed through the production. The first number will be the earliest item number given to the figurine.

67626	Angel leaning against column, candleholder	☐
67627, 77908	Ornament Angel in ring	☐
67628, 77907	Angel standing, holding bunny	☐
67630, 77906	Angel kneeling candleholder	☐
67631, 77905	Angel sitting, votive	☐
69475, 77909	Four Inch Ornament Angel/stars, sitting	☐
69475, 77909	Four Inch Ornament Angel/flying	☐
69475, 77909	Four Inch Ornament Angel/sitting with legs crossed	☐
69475, 77909	Four Inch Ornament Angel/standing, star, garland	☐
76745	Angel holding bunny	☐
76746	Angel with lion and lamb frame	☐
77905	Angel votive	☐
77910	Angel standing with arms reaching out	☐

Sec. Mkt.: $25 - $100

_____ Have _____ Want _____ Paid

Retired Charming Tails

1994

87184	Baby's First Christmas
87924	Binkey On Ice
87187	Binkey's Snack
89317	Bunny with Carrot
85399	Cornfield Feast
89316	Duckling In Egg with Mouse
89315	Duckling Votive
87971	Friends In Flight
89307	Hide And Seek
87188	Lady Bug Express
87518	Letter To Santa
89314	Love Mice
87191	Mackenzie Blowing Bubbles
87187	Mackenzie's Snack
87956	Mini Surprise
85400	Mouse Facing Away
84525	Mouse In Apple Box Set
89191	Mouse on Bee
89320	Mouse On Dragonfly
89321	Mouse on Grasshopper
85508	Open Pumpkin
85509	Pear Candleholder
85510	Pumpkin Votive
87924	Reginald on Ice
87199	Reginald's Bubble Ride
86790	Rocking Mice Musical
87200	Sailing Away
87517	Sharing The Warmth
87511	Skating Mouse Musical
85516	Stump Behind Leaf
85516	Stump Beside Candleholder
87534	Sweet Dreams Waterglobe
87530	Together At Christmas
87516	Trimming For The Tree

1995

87032	Apple House Lighted
89605	Binkey Growing Carrots
87572	Binkey's 1995 Ice Sculpture
87038	Bunny Crystal Bell
89606	Butterfly Smells Zinnia
89607	Chauncey Growing Tomatoes
86787	Chickadees on Ball
86791	Chicks with Bead Garland
86789	Fresh Fruit, Mackenzie
86789	Fresh Fruit, Belle
86789	Fresh Fruit, Binkey
85507	Harvest Fruit, Binkey
85507	Harvest Fruit, Chauncey
87992	High Flying Mackenzie
87969	Holiday Lights Ornament
87939	Holiday Wreath, Binkey
87939	Holiday Wreath, Mackenzie
87993	Hot Doggin'
87542	Jawbreakers Musical
87519	Leaf Vine Ornament Hanger
89604	Mackenzie Growing Beans
87925	Mackenzie & Maxine Caroling
87940	Mackenzie Napping
87942	Maxine Lights A Candle
89555	Me Next!
86786	Mice In Leaf Sleigh
86788	Mice on Glass Ball
87506	Mice On Vine Basket
87189	Mouse Candle Climber
85400	Mouse Candleholder
87501	Mouse Card Holder
87038	Mouse Crystal Bell
87502	Mouse In A Treehole
87529	Mouse On Basket
92224	Mouse On Cheese
87503	Mouse On Leaf
92225	Mouse On Rubber Duck
87037	Mouse On Snowflake
87504	Mouse On Vine
87505	Mouse On Vine Wreath
87045	Mouse On Yellow Bulb
87598	Mouse Star Treetop

87044	Mouse With Apple Facing Away from Candle	98417	Feeding Time
87044	Mouse With Apple Facing Candle	87305	Flying Leaf Saucer
		85511	Frosting Pumpkins
89557	My Hero!	85608	Giving Thanks
87027	Pear House Lighted	85398	Gourd Slide
87036	Porcelain Mouse Bell	87584	Great Oak Town Hall
85778	Pumpkin Playtime	87941	Hang In There
85513	Pumpkin Slide	87299	Holiday Balloon Ride
87509	Pyramid With Mice	85610	Horn Of Plenty
86788	Rabbit on Glass Ball, Holly	87202	Horsing Around
89312	Rabbit with Daffodil	98461	How Do You Measure Love
87308	Stewart At Play	89559	Jelly Bean Feast
87307	Stewart's Winter Fun, Icicle	89318	King Of The Mushroom
87307	Stewart's Winter Fun, Snowflake	87947	Leaf Fence
		87192	Mackenzie Bubble Ride
87186	The Grape Escape, Binkey	87970	Mackenzie on Ice
87186	The Grape Escape, Mackenzie	87560	Mail Box, Bench
		87573	Mail Mouse
89556	Underwater Explorer	87185	Maxine & Mackenzie
89602	Up, Up, And Away	87510	Maxine Making Snow Angels
		89190	Maxine's Butterfly Ride
		87430	Maxine's Pumpkin Costume
		98460	Mender Of Broken Hearts
		87532	Our First Chrismas 1996

1996

		85514	Painting Leaves
		87565	Pear Taxi
		89753	Peek-A-Boo
		87522	Pumpkin Inn
85403	Acorn Built For Two	85606	Pumpkin Pie
87948	Acorn St. Lamp	85777	Reginald's Hideaway
87498	All I Can Give You Is Me	89560	Slumber Party
87476	All Snug In Their Beds	87512	Snack For The Reindeer
87486	All Snug In Their Beds	87566	Snow Plow
89313	Animals In Eggs, Bunny	89310	Spring Flowers, Blue Flower
89313	Animals In Eggs, Duck	89310	Spring Flowers, Yellow Flower
89313	Animals In Eggs, Mouse		
89313	Animals In Eggs, Chick	89563	Springtime Showers, Binkey
87475	Baby's First Christmas	89563	Springtime Showers, Mackenzie
89305	Binkey In a Lily		
87426	Binkey In Bed Of Flowers	89563	Springtime Showers, Reginald
89752	Binkey In Berry Patch		
89586	Binkey's New Pal	87991	Sticky Situations, Mouse on Candy Cane
87580	Binkey's Snow Shoeing		
85611	Candy Apples	87991	Sticky Situations, Ribbon Candy
85607	Candy Corn Vampire		
85402	Caps Off To You	87691	Take Me Home
87583	Carrot Post Office	87571	Teamwork Helps!
87521	Chestnut Chapel	89754	Thanks For Being There
89615	Easter Parade	87570	The Snowball Fight
85401	Fall Frolicking, Under Leaf	89306	Two Peas In A Pod
85401	Fall Frolicking, Under Mushroom	98929	You Are Not Alone
		87472	You Melted My Heart

1997

	Acorn Society	87386	The Chase Is On
89558	After Lunch Snooze	86784	The Drifters
87698	Airmail	86784	The Drifters
87703	All The Trimmings	87366	This Is Hot!
87705	Baby's First Christmas 1997	87398	Training Wings
98349	Binkey's First Cake	87379	Want A Bite?
87303	Binkey's Poinsettia	87493	Weeeeeee!
86785	Catching ZZZ's		
87590	Extra! Extra!		

Limited Editions

87492	Fallen Angel
87490	Flights of Fancy
87492	Frequent Flyer
85615	Garden Naptime
97719	Get Well Soon
87367	Hello, Sweet Pea
97723	Hope You're Feeling Better
87425	Hoppity Hop
87390	I'm Berry Happy
87365	I'm Full
97721	It's Not The Same Without You
87513	Jingle Bells
85512	Jumpin' Jack -O-Lanterns
85776	Let's Get Crackin
87486	Letter To Santa
87373	Look Out Below
86704	Mackenzie in a mitten
86709	Mackenzie's Jack In The Box
87300	Mackenzie's Whirlygig
87500	My New Toy
87360	One For Me...
87361	One For You.....
87469	OOPS! Did I Do That
86708	Our First Christmas
87527	Peeking At Presents
87438	Pickin' Time
87369	Picking Peppers
87302	Reginald In Leaves, Racoon Parachuting
87302	Reginald in Leaves, Racoon Riding Leaf
87591	Reginald's Newstand
87353	Surrounded By Friends
87399	Taggin' Along
87396	Take Time to Reflect
87514	Testing The Lights
87391	The Berry Best

87703	All The Trimmings
87471	All Wrapped Up
87850	Baby's First Christmas
87422	Binkey's Bouncing Bundle
89600	Can I Keep HIm
87611	Candy Apple Candy Store
89601	Fragile Handle With Care
98197	I Picked This Just For You
87306	l995 Annual Ornament Stocking
87944	Mackenzie Snowball
98196	Mackenzie The snowman
89562	Maxine Picking Strawberries, Mouse In Strawberry
87569	Sleigh Ride
87362	Tuggin' Two-some
89561	Wanna Play?

Alphabetical Index

2 Bunnies, Eggcup	63606	114
1995 Annual Ornament, Stocking	87306	60

A

A Collection Of Friends	.98208	101
A Day At The Lake	.83803	26
A Growing Friendship	.97/12	97
A Little Bird Told Me So	.89720	14
A Special Delivery	.86707	49
Acorn Built For Two	.85403	37
Acorn Leaf Candleholder	.86874	109
Acorn Society		96
Acorn St. Lamp	.87948	77
After Lunch Snooze	.89558	8
After The Hunt	.87372	18
Ahhh-Chooo!	.89624	12
Air Mail To Santa	.86652	47
Airmail	.87698	84
All I Can Give You Is Me	.87498	81
All Lit Up Lighted Ornament	.86660	48
All Snug In Their Beds	.87486	91
All Snug In Their Beds	.87476	91
All The Trimmings	.87703	85
All Wrapped Up	.87471	80
Angel Of Light	.87481	66
Animals In Eggs, Bunny	.89313	20
Animals In Eggs, Duck	.89313	20
Animals In Eggs, Mouse	.89313	21
Animals In Eggs, Yellow Chick	.89313	20
Apple House Lighted	.87032	52
Asleep Bunny	.89411	113
Awake Bunny	.89411	112

B

Baby's First Christmas, 1994	.87184	54
Baby's First Christmas, 1997	.87705	85
Baby's First Christmas, 1996	.87850	76
Baby's First Christmas, Waterglobe	87475	90
Bag Of Tricks ....Or Treats	.87436	34
Basket Of Bunnies	.88545	110
Basket With Diapers	.63095	114
Bear Marble Ornament	.69243	116
Bear On Candy Cane	.69422	118
Bear On Glass Ball Ornament	.69337	115
Bear On Holly Leaf	.69423	118
Bear On Snowflake	.69421	117
Bear Thimble Ornament	.69264	117
Bearing Gifts	.87600	84
Binkey Growing Carrots	.89605	23
Binkey In a Lily	.89305	6
Binkey In Bed Of Flowers	.87426	79
Binkey In Berry Patch	.89752	24
Binkey On Ice	.87924	86
Binkey's Acorn Costume	.87429	33
Binkey's Bouncing Bundle	.87422	19
Binkey's First Cake	.98349	17
Binkey's 1995 Ice Sculpture	.87572	73
Binkey's New Pal	.89586	10
Binkey's Poinsettia	.87303	60
Binkey's Snack	.87187	56
Binkey's Snow Shoeing	.87580	83
Bird On Ice Cube Ornament	.69186	115
Booo!	.85417	38
Boy Bunny On Flower	.63605	114
Building A Snowbunny	.87692	84
Building Castles	.83802	26
Bundle Of Joy	.86655	47
Bunny Basket Trinket Box	.89408	112
Bunny Buddies	.89619	11
Bunny Buddies, Musical	.41454125	105
Bunny Bunch of Flowers	.88791	111
Bunny Butterfly Candleholders	.89411	112
Bunny Butterfly Candleholders	.89411	113
Bunny Crystal Bell	87038	53
Bunny Daffodil Egg	88792	113
Bunny Doctor	63613	114
Bunny Egg Topper	88546	110
Bunny Fireman	63614	114
Bunny Imposter	89609	23
Bunny In Teacup	63649	114
Bunny Iris Egg	88792	113
Bunny Love	87424	19
Bunny Trio	88794	112
Bunny With Carrot Candleholder	89317	21
Butterfly Smells Zinnia	89606	23
Butternut Squash Dairy	87562	72

C

Camping Out	83703	25
Can I Keep Him	89600	22
Candy Apple Candy Store	87611	74
Candy Apples	85611	32
Candy Cane Birdhouse Ornament	69195	115
Candy Corn Vampire	85607	32
Cantaloupe Cathederal	87597	74
Caps Off To You	85402	36
Carrot Post Office	87583	73
Cat With Button	69612	118
Catchin' Butterflies	87423	4
Catchin' Butterflies, Musical	41451108	104
Catching ZZZ's	86785	50
Cattail Catapult	87448	5
Charming Choo-Choo & Caboose	87579	68
Charming Tails Display Sign	87690	76

125

Title	Number	Page
Chauncey's Choo-Choo	87707	69
Chauncey's First Christmas	86710	49
Chauncey's Growing Tomatoes	89607	23
Chauncey's Noisemakers	87554	44
Chauncey's Pear Costume	87431	33
Chestnut Chapel	87521	70
Chickadees On Ball	86787	51
Chickie Back Ride	88700	20
Chicks with Bead Garland	86791	52
Chipmunk Blowing Bubbles	67388	115
Chipmunk Holly Leaf	69423	118
Chipmunk In Walnut	69618	119
Chipmunk Marble Ornament	69243	116
Chipmunk On Acorn	69619	120
Chipmunk On Candy Cane	69422	118
Chipmunk Snowflake	69421	117
Chipmunk Stocking Holder		119
Chipmunk Thimble Ornament	69264	117
Christmas Cookies, Binkey	87301	59
Christmas Cookies, Mackenzie	87301	59
Christmas Cookies, Reginald	87301	58
Christmas Flowers	87304	60
Christmas Pageant Stage	87546	66
Christmas Stamps	87485	62
Christmas Stroll	87575	45
Christmas Trio	87713	46
Come On In The Water's Fine	83804	27
Cornfield Feast	85399	35
Cowboy Bunny	63616	114

D

Title	Number	Page
Dashing Through The Snow	87624	75
Decorating Binkey	87714	85
DIET?...TOMORRROW	67319	117
Dog In Thimble	69613	119
Duckling In Egg with Mouse	89316	21
Duckling Votive	89315	21

E

Title	Number	Page
Easter Egg Candleholder	88787	111
Easter Egg Trinket Box	89409	112
Easter Parade	89615	23
Even The Ups And Downs	89705	13
Everyday	81/1-4	103
Everyone Needs A Hand, Extra! Extra!	87590	74

F

Title	Number	Page
Fall and the Squashville Christmas Parade	81/1	103
Fall and the Squashville Christmas Parade Harvest	81/1	103
Fall and the Squashville Christmas Parade, Harvest, Winter Holiday, Variety, Spring and Fall Frolicking, Under a Leaf	85401	36
Fall Frolicking, Under a Mushroom	85401	36
Fallen Angel	87492	62
Farmer Mackenzie	87695	84
Feeding Time	98417	24
Flights Of Fancy	87490	62
Flower Friends	89608	11
Flying Leaf Saucer	87305	79
Follow In My Footsteps	87473	44
Four Chipmunks Yawning Waterglobe	64238	115
Fox Holly Leaf	69423	118
Fox Marble Ornament	69243	116
Fox On Candy Cane	69422	118
Fox On Snowflake	69421	117
Fox Thimble Ornament	69264	117
Fragile Handle With Care	89601	10
Frequent Flyer	87492	62
Fresh Fruit, Belle	86789	52
Fresh Fruit, Binkey	86789	51
Fresh Fruit, Mackenzie	86789	51
Friends In Flight	87971	89
Frog Marble Ornament	69243	116
Frog Thimble Ornament	69264	117
Frosting Pumpkins	85511	39

G

Title	Number	Page
Garden Naptime	85615	41
Gathering Treats	87377	18
Get Well Soon	97719	15
Ghost Stories	85703	32
Girl Bunny on Flower	63605	114
Giving Thanks	85608	40
Gone Fishin'	83702	25
Good Luck	97716	15
Gourd Slide	85398	35
Great Oak Town Hall	87584	73
Guess What!	89714	78

H

Title	Number	Page
Halloween		106
Hang In There	87941	87
Hang On	98600	101
Hangin' Around	89623	11
Hangin' Around Musical	41451231	105
Happy Birthday	97715	15
Harvest Fruit, Binkey	85507	38
Harvest Fruit, Chauncey	85507	38
Heading For The Slopes	86656	47
Hear, Speak, See No Evil	89717	14
Hello, Sweet Pea	87367	2
Here Comes The Bride	82100	28
Hide And Seek	89307	6
High Flying Mackenzie	87992	65
Holiday Balloon Ride	87299	58
Holiday Lights Ornament	87969	88
Holiday Trumpeter	87555	44
Holiday Wreath, Binkey	87939	86
Holiday Wreath, Mackenzie	87939	86
Holy Family Players	87547	67
Hope You're Feeling Better	97723	16
Hoppity Hop	87425	4
Horn Of Plenty	85610	40
Horsing Around	87202	58

Hot Doggin'	87993	77	Mackenzie & Maxine Caroling	87925	76
How Do You Measure Love	98461	17	Mackenzie Napping	87940	87
How Many Candles	89713	13	Mackenzie On Ice	87970	88
			Mackenzie Snowball	87944	88

I

			Mackenzie The Snowman	98196	99
I Have A Question For You	89603	11	Mackenzie's Jack In The Box 1997	86709	49
I Love You	97724	17	Mackenzie's Snack	87187	56
I Love You A Whole Bunch	89715	78	Mackenzie's Whirlygig	87300	58
I' m A Winner	89719	14	Maid Of Honor	82102	28
I Picked This Just For You	98197	99	Mail Box, Bench	87560	71
I See Things Clearly Now	89626	12	Mail Mouse	87573	73
I'm Berry Happy	87390	3	Manger Animals	87482	66
I'm Berry Happy, Musical	41454090	105	Maxine Goes On Line	89702	78
I'm Full	87365	2	Maxine Lights A Candle	87942	88
I'm Here For You	89706	13	Maxine & Mackenzie	87185	55
I'm So Sorry	97720	16	Maxine & Mackenzie	87185	55
I'm Thinking Of You	89701	78	Maxine Making Snow Angels	87510	82
Indian Imposter	87446	43	Maxine Picking Strawberries,		
It's Not The Same Without You	97721	16	Mouse in Strawberry	89562	99
It's Your Move	89704	13	Maxine's Angel	86701	48
			Maxine's Butterfly Ride	89190	5
			Maxine's Leaf Collection,		

J

Jack O'Lantern Jalopy	85410	37	1997 Charter Members Only	98701	96
Jawbreakers Musical	87542	92	Maxine's Pumpkin Costume	87430	33
Jelly Bean Feast	89559	22	Maxine's Snowmobile Ride	87612	84
Jingle Bells	87513	82	Me Next!	89555	93
Jumpin' Jack -O-Lanterns	85512	31	Mender Of Broken Hearts	98460	17
			Merry Christmas From Our House		
			To Yours	87622	75

K

Keeping Our Love Alive	89710	78	Mice In Leaf Sleigh	86786	50
King Of The Mushroom	89318	8	Mice on Glass Ball/Holly	86788	51
			Mice On Vine Basket	87506	64
			Midday Snooze	89617	11

L

			Midday Snooze, Musical	41451223	104
L'il Drummer Mouse	87480	66	Mini Surprise, Waterglobe	87956	93
Lady Bug Express	87188	56	Mouse Candle Climber	87189	57
Leaf Fence	87947	77	Mouse Candleholder	85400	35
Leaf Vine Ornament Hanger	87519	102	Mouse Candleholder, Facing Away	85400	36
Let's Get Crackin	85776	41	Mouse Card Holder	87501	81
Letter To Santa	87486	62	Mouse Crystal Bell	87038	54
Letter To Santa	87518	92	Mouse In A Treehole		
Life Is A Bed Of Roses	98198	100	Candleholder	87502	63
Life's A Picnic With You	83701	25	Mouse In Apple Box Set Of 3	84525	5
Little Drummer Boy	87557	45	Mouse On Basket	87529	65
Little Lamb Egg Topper	88560	111	Mouse On Bee	89191	5
Look! No Hands	87428	33	Mouse On Cheese Waterglobe	92224	94
Look Out Below	87373	18	Mouse On Dragonfly	89320	8
Love Blooms	87862	98	Mouse On Grasshopper	89321	8
Love Me - Love Me Not	87395	3	Mouse On Leaf Candleholder	87503	63
Love Mice	89314	7	Mouse On Rubber Duck		
			Waterglobe	92225	94

M

			Mouse On Snowflake	87037	53
Machenzie's Holiday Hat	98202	100	Mouse On Vine Candleholder	87504	63
Mackenzie Blowing Bubbles	87191	57	Mouse On Vine Wreath	87505	64
Mackenzie Bubble Ride	87192	57	Mouse On Yellow Bulb	87045	54
Mackenzie Building Snowmouse	87203	79	Mouse Star Treetop	87598	83
Mackenzie Growing Beans	89604	22	Mouse With Apple Candleholder,		
Mackenzie In A Mitten	86704	49	Facing Away From Candle	87044	42

Entry	Number	Page
Mouse With Apple Candleholder, Facing Candle	87044	42
Mushroom Depot	87563	72
My Heart's All A Flutter (Groom)	82101	28
My Hero!	89557	94
My New Toy	87500	81
My Spring Bonnet	98204	100

N

Entry	Number	Page
New Arrival	97717	15
No Thanks, I'm Stuffed	88603	19
Not A Creature Was Stirring	87704	76

O

Entry	Number	Page
Old Cob Mill	87524	70
One For Me...	87360	1
One For You.....	87361	1
One Mouse Open Sleigh	98195	99
OOPS! Did I Do That	87469	80
Oops! I Missed	87443	42
Open Pumpkin	85508	31
Opossum Marble Ornament	69243	116
Our First Chrismas l996	87532	65
Our First Christmas	86708	49
Our First Christmas Together, 3rd Edition	86653	47

P

Entry	Number	Page
Paint By Paws	88701	20
Painting Leaves	85514	39
Parade Banner	87543	44
Pear Candleholder	85509	38
Pear House Lighted	87027	52
Pear Taxi	87565	72
Peek-A-Boo	89753	24
Peek-A-Boo In The Posies	98200	100
Peeking At Presents	87527	82
Peppermint Bears		107
Peppermint Party, Holding Mint	87314	61
Peppermint Party, Upside Down	87314	61
Pickin' Time	87438	42
Picking Peppers	87369	3
Picture Perfect	89722	14
Pig On Ear Of Corn	69617	119
Pilgrim's Progress	87445	43
Pine Cone Predicament l998	86659	48
Pink Columbine Ornament Hanger	89610	102
Plane Friends	89627	12
Playing Bunnies Egg Holder	63610	114
Please, Just One More	87625	76
Police Bunny	63615	114
Porcelain Mouse Bell	87036	53
Pumpkin Inn	87522	70
Pumpkin Pie	85606	40
Pumpkin Playtime	85778	90
Pumpkin Slide	85513	39
Pumpkin Votive	85510	31
Pumpkin's First Pumpkin	85411	37

Entry	Number	Page
Pyramid With Mice Candleholder	87509	64

R

Entry	Number	Page
Rabbit On Glass Ball, Holly	86788	51
Rabbit With Daffodil	89312	7
Raccoon In Walnut	69618	120
Racoon On Acorn	69619	120
Reach For The Stars	97718	15
Reach For The Stars/Musical	4145095	104
Reginald in Leaves, Racoon Parachuting	87302	59
Reginald in Leaves, Racoon Riding Leaf	87302	59
Reginald On Ice	87924	86
Reginald's Bubble Ride	87199	57
Reginald's Choo-Choo Ride	87620	68
Reginald's Gourd Costume	85701	32
Reginald's Hideaway	85777	41
Reginald's Newstand	87591	74
Rocking Mice Musical	86790	90
Row Boat Romance	83801	26

S

Entry	Number	Page
Sailing Away	87200	90
Santa Tangled In Lights Ornament	69244	116
Sending A Little Snow Your Way	87601	98
Sharing The Warmth	87517	91
Shepherd's Set	87710	67
Skating Mouse Musical	87511	91
Ski Jumper	86657	48
Skunk With Bubbles	69488	115
Sleigh Ride	87569	72
Slumber Party	89560	9
Small Bunny Candleholder	88543	110
Small Carrot Candleholder	89412	113
Snack For The Reindeer	87512	65
Snow Makers	52571	108
Snow Plow	87566	82
Spring And Every Day Lazy Days	81/2	103
Spring And Every Day Garden	81/2	103
Spring and Every Day Potting Shed	81/2	103
Spring Flowers, Blue Flower	89310	7
Spring Flowers, Yellow Flower	89310	6
Springtime Flowers, Yellow Musical	4147023100	105
Springtime Showers, Binkey	89563	9
Springtime Showers, Mackenzie	89563	9
Springtime Showers, Reginald	89563	9
Squash Gourd Candleholder	86885	109
Squirrel Bubbles	69489	115
Squirrel Marble Ornament	69243	116
Stack O' Lanterns	85416	38
Stag Candleholder	51605	109
Stamp Dispenser	87483	80
Steady Wins The Race	89716	14
Stewart At Play	87308	61
Stewart's Apple Costume	85700	32
Stewart's Choo-Choo Ride	87694	69
Stewart's Day In The Sun	83805	27

Entry	Item #	Page
Stewart's Winter Fun, Icicle	.87307	61
Stewart's Winter Fun, Snowflake	.87307	60
Sticky Situations, Mouse on Candy Cane	.87991	89
Sticky Situations, Ribbon Candy	.87991	89
Street Light, Sign	.87561	71
Stump Candleholder Behind Leaf	.85516	40
Stump Candleholder Beside Candleholder	.85516	39
Surrounded By Friends	.87353	1
Sweet Dreams Waterglobe	.87534	92

𝒯

Entry	Item #	Page
Taggin' Along	.87399	4
Take Me Home	.87691	98
Take Time To Reflect	.87396	4
Teacher's Pets	.89700	78
Team Igloo	.87623	75
Teamwork Helps!	.87571	83
Testing The Lights	.87514	70
Thank You	.98700	96
Thanks For Being There	.89754	24
Thanks For Being There, Musical	41470249	105
The Altar Of Love	.82108	29
The Berry Best	.87391	3
The Best Bunny	.82103	28
The Blossom Bounce	.83704	26
The Chase Is On	.87386	19
The Drifters	.86784	50
The Drum Major	.87556	45
The Float Driver	.87587	45
The Gardening Break	.87364	2
The Get Away Car	.82107	29
The Good Witch	.85704	33
The Grape Escape, Binkey	.87186	55
The Grape Escape, Mackenzie	.87186	55
The Ring Bearer	.82104	29
The Santa Balloon	.87708	46
The Snowball Fight	.87570	83
The Waterslide	.87384	3
There's No "Us" Without "U"	.89703	12
This Is Hot!	.87366	2
Three Leaf Candleholder	.86867	109
Three Wise Mice	.87548	67
Toasting Marshmallows	.83700	25
Together At Christmas	.87530	92
Together Forever	.82109	30
Town Crier	.87696	46
Training Wings	.87398	4
Tricycle Built From Treats	.86658	48
Trimming For The Tree Waterglobe	.87516	91
Trimming The Tree	.87702	85
Tuggin' Two-some	.87362	2
Turkey Traveller	.85702	41
Turkey With Dressing	.85412	37
Two Peas In A Pod	.89306	6

𝒰

Entry	Item #	Page
Underwater Explorer	.89556	93
Up, Up, And Away	.89602	94

𝒱

Entry	Item #	Page
Variety Garden	.81/4	103
Variety Potting Shed	.81/4	103
Variety Winter In The Park	.81/4	103
Village Sign	.87533	71

𝒲

Entry	Item #	Page
Waiting For Christmas	.87496	81
Wanna Play?	.89561	22
Want A Bite?	.87379	18
Waterslide Musical	.41450182	104
We'll Weather The Storm	.97722	16
Wedding Day Blossoms	.82105	29
Weeeeeee!	.87493	63
What's Hatchin'?	.88600	19
Who Put That Tree There?	.87621	75
Why Hello There	.87357	1
Winter Holiday Nativity	.81/3	103
Winter Holiday Train Station	.81/3	103
Winter Holiday Winter In The Park	.81/3	103
Woodpecker On Cookie Ornament	.69207	116

𝒴

Entry	Item #	Page
Yellow Duck Egg Topper	.88555	110
Yellow Lily Ornament Hanger	.89611	102
You Are Not Alone	.98929	101
You Couldn't Be Sweeter	.89625	12
You Melted My Heart	.87472	80
You're Not Scary	.87440	34
You're Nutty	.87451	43

Item Number Index

Series	Entry	Page
	Acorn Society	.96
	Chipmunk Stocking Holder	.119
	Halloween	.106
	Peppermint Bears	.107
81/1	Fall And the Squashville Christmas Parade	.103
81/1	Fall And The Squashville Christmas Parade Harvest	.103
81/2	Spring And Every DayLazy Days	.103
81/2	Spring And Everyday Garden	.103
81/2	Spring And Everyday Potting Shed	103
81/3	Winter Holiday Nativity	.103
81/3	Winter Holiday Train Station	.103
81/3	Winter Holiday Winter In The Park	103
81/4	Variety Garden	.103
81/4	Variety Potting Shed	.103
81/4	Variety Winter In The Park	.103

#	Title	Page	#	Title	Page
97/12	A Growing Friendship	97	83803	A Day At The Lake	26
51605	Stag Candleholder	109	83804	Come On In The Water's Fine	27
52571	Snow Makers	108	83805	Stewart's Day In The Sun	27
63095	Basket With Diapers	114	84525	Mouse In Apple Box Set Of 3	5
63605	Boy Bunny On Flower	114	85398	Gourd Slide	35
63605	Girl Bunny On Flower	114	85399	Cornfield Feast	35
63606	2 Bunnies, Eggcup	114	85400	Mouse Candleholder	35
63610	Playing Bunnies Egg Holder	114	85400	Mouse Candleholder, Facing Away	36
63613	Bunny Doctor	114	85401	Fall Frolicking, Under a Leaf	36
63614	Bunny Fireman	114	85401	Fall Frolicking, Under a Mushroom	36
63615	Police Bunny	114	85402	Caps Off To You	36
63616	Cowboy Bunny	114	85403	Acorn Built For Two	37
63649	Bunny In Teacup	114	85410	Jack O'Lantern Jalopy	37
64238	Four Chipmunks Yawning	115	85411	Pumpkin's First Pumpkin	37
67319	DIET?...TOMORRROW	117	85412	Turkey With Dressing	37
67388	Chipmunk Blowing Bubbles	115	85416	Stack O' Lanterns	38
69186	Bird On Ice Cube Ornament	115	85417	Booo!	38
69195	Candy Cane Birdhouse Ornament	115	85507	Harvest Fruit, Binkey	38
69207	Woodpecker On Cookie Ornament	116	85507	Harvest Fruit, Chauncey	38
69243	Bear Marble Ornament	116	85508	Open Pumpkin	31
69243	Chipmunk Marble Ornament	116	85509	Pear Candleholder	38
69243	Fox Marble Ornament	116	85510	Pumpkin Votive	31
69243	Frog Marble Ornament	116	85511	Frosting Pumpkins	39
69243	Opossum Marble Ornament	116	85512	Jumpin' Jack-O-Lanterns	31
69243	Squirrel Marble Ornament	116	85513	Pumpkin slide	39
69244	Santa Tangled In Lights Ornament	116	85514	Painting Leaves	39
69264	Bear Thimble Ornament	117	85516	Stump Candleholder Behind Leaf	40
69264	Chipmunk Thimble Ornament	117	85516	Stump Candleholder Beside Candleholder	39
69264	Fox Thimble Ornament	117	85606	Pumpkin Pie	40
69264	Frog Thimble Ornament	117	85607	Candy Corn Vampire	32
69337	Bear On Glass Ball Ornament	115	85608	Giving Thanks	40
69421	Bear On Snowflake	117	85610	Horn Of Plenty	40
69421	Chipmunk Snowflake	117	85611	Candy Apples	32
69421	Fox On Snowflake	117	85615	Garden Naptime	41
69422	Bear On Candy Cane	118	85700	Stewart's Apple Costume	32
69422	Chipmunk On Candy Cane	118	85701	Reginald's Gourd Costume	32
69422	Fox On Candy Cane	118	85702	Turkey Traveller	41
69423	Bear On Holly Leaf	118	85703	Ghost Stories	32
69423	Chipmunk Holly Leaf	118	85704	The Good Witch	33
69423	Fox Holly Leaf	118	85776	Let's Get Crackin	41
69488	Skunk With Bubbles	115	85777	Reginald's Hideaway	41
69489	Squirrel Bubbles	115	85778	Pumpkin Playtime	90
69612	Cat With Button	118	86652	Air Mail To Santa	47
69613	Dog In Thimble	119	86653	Our First Christmas Together 3rd Edition	47
69617	Pig On Ear Of Corn	119	86655	Bundle Of Joy	47
69618	Chipmunk In Walnut	119	86656	Heading For The Slopes	47
69618	Raccoon In Walnut	120	86657	Ski Jumper	48
69619	Chipmunk On Acorn	120	86658	Tricycle Built From Treats	48
69619	Racoon On Acorn	120	86659	Pine Cone Predicament 1998	48
82100	Here Comes The Bride	28	86660	All Lit Up Lighted Ornament	48
82101	My Heart's All A Flutter (Groom)	28	86701	Maxine's Angel	48
82102	Maid Of Honor	28	86704	Mackenzie In A Mitten	49
82103	The Best Bunny	28	86707	A Special Delivery	49
82104	The Ring Bearer	29	86708	Our First Christmas	49
82105	Wedding Day Blossoms	29	86709	Mackenzie's Jack In The Box 1997	49
82107	The Get Away Car	29	86710	Chauncey's First Christmas	49
82108	The Altar Of Love	29	86784	The Drifters	50
82109	Together Forever	30	86785	Catching ZZZ's	50
83700	Toasting Marshmallows	25	86786	Mice In Leaf Sleigh	50
83701	Life's A Picnic With You	25	86787	Chickadees On Ball	51
83702	Gone Fishin'	25	86788	Mice On Glass Ball, Holly	51
83703	Camping Out	25	86788	Rabbit On Glass Ball, Holly	51
83704	The Blossom Bounce	26	86789	Fresh Fruit, Belle	52
83801	Row Boat Romance	26			
83802	Building Castles	26			

86789	Fresh Fruit, Binkey ... .51	87386	The Chase Is On ... .19
86789	Fresh Fruit, Mackenzie ... .51	87390	I'm Berry Happy 3
86790	Rocking Mice Musical ... .90	87391	The Berry Best 3
86791	Chicks With Bead Garland ... .52	87395	Love Me -Love Me Not 3
86867	Three Leaf Candleholder ... .109	87396	Take Time To Reflect 4
86874	Acorn Leaf Candleholder ... .109	87398	Training Wings 4
86885	Squash Gourd Candleholder ... .109	87399	Taggin' Along 4
87027	Pear House Lighted ... .52	87422	Binkey's Bouncing Bundle ... .19
87032	Apple House Lighted ... .52	87423	Catchin' Butterflies 4
87036	Porcelain Mouse Bell ... .53	87424	Bunny Love ... .19
87037	Mouse On Snowflake ... .53	87425	Hoppity Hop 4
87038	Bunny Crystal Bell ... .53	87426	Binkey In Bed Of Flowers ... .79
87038	Mouse Crystal Bell ... .54	87428	Look! No Hands ... .33
87044	Mouse With Apple Candleholder, Facing Away from Candle ... .42	87429	Binkey's Acorn Costume ... .33
		87430	Maxine's Pumpkin Costume ... .33
87044	Mouse With Apple Candleholder, Facing Candle ... .42	87431	Chauncey's Pear Costume ... .33
		87436	Bag Of Tricks ....Or Treats ... .34
87045	Mouse On Yellow Bulb ... .54	87438	Pickin' Time ... .42
87184	Baby's First Christmas, 1994 ... .54	87440	You're Not Scary ... .34
87185	Maxine & Mackenzie ... .55	87443	Oops! I Missed ... .42
87185	Maxine & Mackenzie ... .55	87445	Pilgrim's Progress ... .43
87186	The Grape Escape, Binkey ... .55	87446	Indian Imposter ... .43
87186	The Grape Escape, Mackenzie ... .55	87448	Cattail Catapult 5
87187	Binkey's Snack ... .56	87451	You're Nutty ... .43
87187	Mackenzie's Snack ... .56	87469	OOPS! Did I Do That ... .80
87188	Lady Bug Express ... .56	87471	All Wrapped Up ... .80
87189	Mouse Candle Climber ... .57	87472	You Melted My Heart ... .80
87191	Mackenzie Blowing Bubbles ... .57	87473	Follow In My Footsteps ... .44
87192	Mackenzie Bubble Ride ... .57	87475	Baby's First Christmas, Waterglobe .90
87199	Reginald's Bubble Ride ... .57	87476	All Snug In Their Beds ... .91
87200	Sailing Away ... .90	87480	L'il Drummer Mouse ... .66
87202	Horsing Around ... .58	87481	Angel Of Light ... .66
87203	Mackenzie Building Snowmouse ... .79	87482	Manger Animals ... .66
87299	Holiday Balloon Ride ... .58	87483	Stamp Dispenser ... .80
87300	Mackenzie's Whirlygig ... .58	87485	Christmas Stamps ... .62
87301	Christmas Cookies, Binkey ... .59	87486	All Snug In Their Beds ... .91
87301	Christmas Cookies, Mackenzie ... .59	87486	Letter To Santa ... .62
87301	Christmas Cookies, Reginald ... .58	87490	Flights of Fancy ... .62
87302	Reginald In Leaves, Racoon parachuting ... .59	87492	Fallen Angel ... .62
		87492	Frequent Flyer ... .62
87302	Reginald In Leaves, Racoon Riding Leaf ... .59	87493	Weeeeeee! ... .63
		87496	Waiting For Christmas ... .81
87303	Binkey's Poinsettia ... .60	87498	All I Can Give You Is Me ... .81
87304	Christmas Flowers ... .60	87500	My New Toy ... .81
87305	Flying Leaf Saucer ... .79	87501	Mouse Card Holder ... .81
87306	1995 Annual Ornament, Stocking ... .60	87502	Mouse In A Treehole Candleholder 63
87307	Stewart's Winter Fun, Icicle ... .61	87503	Mouse On Leaf Candleholder ... .63
87307	Stewart's Winter Fun, Snowflake ... .60	87504	Mouse On Vine Candleholder ... .63
87308	Stewart At Play ... .61	87505	Mouse On Vine Wreath ... .64
87314	Peppermint Party, Holding Mint ... .61	87506	Mice On Vine Basket ... .64
87314	Peppermint Party, Upside Down ... .61	87509	Pyramid With Mice Candleholder ... .64
87353	Surrounded By Friends 1	87510	Maxine Making Snow Angels ... .82
87357	Why Hello There 1	87511	Skating Mouse Musical ... .91
87360	One For Me... 1	87512	Snack For The Reindeer ... .65
87361	One For You..... 1	87513	Jingle Bells ... .82
87362	Tuggin' Two-some 2	87514	Testing The Lights ... .70
87364	The Gardening Break 2	87516	Trimming For The Tree Waterglobe 91
87365	I'm Full 2	87517	Sharing The Warmth ... .91
87366	This Is Hot! 2	87518	Letter To Santa ... .92
87367	Hello, Sweet Pea 2	87519	Leaf Vine Ornament Hanger ... .102
87369	Picking Peppers 3	87521	Chestnut Chapel ... .70
87372	After The Hunt ... .18	87522	Pumpkin Inn ... .70
87373	Look Out Below ... .18	87524	Old Cob Mill ... .70
87377	Gathering Treats ... .18	87527	Peeking At Presents ... .82
87379	Want A Bite? ... .18	87529	Mouse On Basket ... .65
87384	The Waterslide 3	87530	Together At Christmas ... .92

#	Title	Page
87532	Our First Chrismas l996	65
87533	Village Sign	71
87534	Sweet Dreams Waterglobe	92
87542	Jawbreakers Musical	92
87543	Parade Banner	44
87546	Christmas Pageant Stage	66
87547	Holy Family Players	67
87548	Three Wise Mice	67
87554	Chauncey's Noisemakers	44
87555	Holiday Trumpeter	44
87556	The Drum Major	45
87557	Little Drummer Boy	45
87560	Mail Box, Bench	71
87561	Street Light, Sign	71
87562	Butternut Squash Dairy	72
87563	Mushroom Depot	72
87565	Pear Taxi	72
87566	Snow Plow	82
87569	Sleigh Ride	72
87570	The Snowball Fight	83
87571	Teamwork Helps!	83
87572	Binkey's l995 Ice Sculpture	73
87573	Mail Mouse	73
87575	Christmas Stroll	45
87579	Charming Choo-Choo & Caboose	68
87580	Binkey's Snow Shoeing	83
87583	Carrot Post Office	73
87584	Great Oak Town Hall	73
87587	The Float Driver	45
87590	Extra! Extra!	74
87591	Reginald's Newstand	74
87597	Cantaloupe Cathedral	74
87598	Mouse Star Treetop	83
87600	Bearing Gifts	84
87601	Sending A Little Snow Your Way	98
87611	Candy Apple Candy Store	74
87612	Maxine's Snowmobile Ride	84
87620	Reginald's Choo-Choo Ride	68
87621	Who Put That Tree There?	75
87622	Merry Christmas From Our House To Yours	75
87623	Team Igloo	75
87624	Dashing Through The Snow	75
87625	Please, Just One More	76
87690	Charming Tails Display Sign	76
87691	Take Me Home	98
87692	Building a Snowbunny	84
87694	Stewart's Choo-Choo Ride	69
87695	Farmer Mackenzie	84
87696	Town Crier	46
87698	Airmail	84
87702	Trimming The Tree	85
87703	All The Trimmings	85
87704	Not A Creature Was Stirring	76
87705	Baby's First Christmas, 1997	85
87707	Chauncey's Choo-Choo	69
87708	The Santa Balloon	46
87710	Shepherd's Set	67
87713	Christmas Trio	46
87714	Decorating Binkey	85
87850	Baby's First Christmas, l996	76
87862	Love Blooms	98
87924	Binkey On Ice	86
87924	Reginald On Ice	86
87925	Mackenzie & Maxine Caroling	76
87939	Holiday Wreath, Binkey	86
87939	Holiday Wreath, Mackenzie	86
87940	Mackenzie Napping	87
87941	Hang In There	87
87942	Maxine Lights A Candle	88
87944	Mackenzie Snowball	88
87947	Leaf Fence	77
87948	Acorn St. Lamp	77
87956	Mini Surprise, Waterglobe	93
87969	Holiday Lights Ornament	88
87970	Mackenzie on Ice	88
87971	Friends In Flight	89
87991	Sticky Situations, Mouse On Candy Cane	89
87991	Sticky Situations, Ribbon Candy	89
87992	High Flying Mackenzie	65
87993	Hot Doggin'	77
88543	Small Bunny Candleholder	110
88545	Basket Of Bunnies	
88546	Bunny Egg Topper	110
88555	Yellow Duck Egg Topper	110
88560	Little Lamb Egg Topper	111
88600	What's Hatchin'?	19
88603	No Thanks, I'm Stuffed	19
88700	Chickie Back Ride	20
88701	Paint By Paws	20
88787	Easter Egg Candleholder	111
88791	Bunny Bunch of Flowers	111
88792	Bunny Daffodil Egg	113
88792	Bunny Iris Egg	113
88794	Bunny Trio	112
89190	Maxine's Butterfly Ride	5
89191	Mouse On Bee	5
89305	Binkey In a Lily	6
89306	Two Peas In A Pod	6
89307	Hide And Seek	6
89310	Spring Flowers, Blue Flower	7
89310	Spring Flowers, Yellow Flower	6
89312	Rabbit With Daffodil	7
89313	Animals In Eggs, Bunny	20
89313	Animals In Eggs, Duck	20
89313	Animals In Eggs, Mouse	21
89313	Animals In Eggs, Yellow Chick	20
89314	Love Mice	7
89315	Duckling Votive	21
89316	Duckling In Egg With Mouse	21
89317	Bunny With Carrot Candleholder	21
89318	King Of The Mushroom	8
89320	Mouse On Dragonfly	8
89321	Mouse On Grasshopper	8
89408	Bunny Basket Trinket Box	112
89409	Easter Egg Trinket Box	112
89411	Bunny Butterfly Candleholders, Asleep Bunny	113
89411	Bunny Butterfly Candleholders, Awake Bunny	112
89412	Small Carrot Candleholder	113
89555	Me Next!	93
89556	Underwater Explorer	93
89557	My Hero!	94
89558	After Lunch Snooze	8
89559	Jelly Bean Feast	22
89560	Slumber Party	9
89561	Wanna Play?	22
89562	Maxine Picking Strawberries, Mouse in Strawberry	99
89563	Springtime Showers, Binkey	9

89563	Springtime Showers, Mackenzie	9
89563	Springtime Showers, Reginald	9
89586	Binkey's New Pal	10
89600	Can I Keep Him	22
89601	Fragile Handle With Care	10
89602	Up, Up, And Away	94
89603	I Have A Question For You	11
89604	Mackenzie Growing Beans	22
89605	Binkey Growing Carrots	23
89606	Butterfly Smells Zinnia	23
89607	Chauncey's Growing Tomatoes	23
89608	Flower Friends	11
89609	Bunny Imposter	23
89610	Pink Columbine Ornament Hanger	102
89611	Yellow Lily Ornament Hanger	102
89615	Easter Parade	23
89617	Midday Snooze	11
89619	Bunny Buddies	11
89623	Hangin' Around	11
89624	Ahhh-Chooo!	12
89625	You Couldn't Be Sweeter	12
89626	I See Things Clearly Now	12
89627	Plane Friends	12
89700	Teacher's Pets	78
89701	I'm Thinking Of You	78
89702	Maxine Goes On Line	78
89703	There's No "Us" Without "U"	12
89704	It's Your Move	13
89705	Even The Ups And Downs	13
89706	I'm Here For You	13
89710	Keeping Our Love Alive	78
89713	How Many Candles	13
89714	Guess What!	78
89715	I Love You A Whole Bunch	78
89716	Steady Wins The Race	14
89717	Hear, Speak, See No Evil	14
89719	I' m A Winner	14
89720	A Little Bird Told Me So	14
89722	Picture Perfect	14
89752	Binkey In Berry Patch	24
89753	Peek-A-Boo	24
89754	Thanks For Being There	24
92224	Mouse On Cheese Waterglobe	94
92225	Mouse On Rubber Duck Waterglobe	94
97715	Happy Birthday	15
97716	Good Luck	15
97717	New Arrival	15
97718	Reach For The Stars	15
97719	Get Well Soon	15
97720	I'm So Sorry	16
97721	It's Not The Same Without You	16
97722	We'll Weather The Storm	16
97723	Hope You're Feeling Better	16
97724	I Love You	17
98195	One Mouse Open Sleigh	99
98196	Mackenzie The Snowman	99
98197	I Picked This Just For You	99
98198	Life Is A Bed Of Roses	100
98200	Peek-A-Boo In The Posies	100
98202	Machenzie's Holiday Hat	100
98204	My Spring Bonnet	100
98208	A Collection Of Friends	101
98349	Binkey's First Cake	17
98417	Feeding Time	24
98460	Mender Of Broken Hearts	17
98461	How Do You Measure Love	17
98600	Hang On	101
98700	Thank You	96
98701	Maxine's Leaf Collection, 1997 Charter Members Only	96
98929	You Are Not Alone	101
81/1-81/4	Fall and the Squashville Christmas Parade, Harvest, Winter Holiday, Variety, Spring and Everyday	103

San Francisco Music Co.

4145095	Reach For The Stars/Musical	104
41450182	Waterslide Musical	104
41451108	Catchin' Butterflies, Musical	104
41451223	Midday Snooze, Musical	104
41451231	Hangin' Around Musical	105
41454090	I'm Berry Happy, Musical	105
41454125	Bunny Buddies, Musical	105
41470249	Everyone Needs A Hand, Thanks For Being There, Musical	105
4147023100	Springtime Flowers Yellow Musical	105

Look for the new Teeny Tiny Tails
Squashville County Fair. Designed by
Dean Griff.
The Big Winner, The Berry Toss Game,
Test Your Strength and The Ticket Booth.

Notes